MACAT

An Analysis of

Baruch Spinoza's

Ethics

Gary Slater
with
Andreas Vrahimis

ROUTLEDGE

Published by Macat International Ltd
24:13 Coda Centre, 189 Munster Road, London SW6 6AW.

Distributed exclusively by Routledge
2 Park Square, Milton Park, Abingdon, Oxon OX14 4RN
711 Third Avenue, New York, NY 10017, USA

Routledge is an imprint of the Taylor & Francis Group, an informa business

Copyright © 2017 by Macat International Ltd
Macat International has asserted its right under the Copyright, Designs and Patents Act
1988 to be identified as the copyright holder of this work.

www.macat.com
info@macat.com

Cataloguing in Publication Data
A catalogue record for this book is available from the British Library.
Library of Congress Cataloguing-in-Publication Data is available upon request.
Cover illustration: Etienne Gilfillan

ISBN 978-1-912303-14-4 (hardback)
ISBN 978-1-912127-03-0 (paperback)
ISBN 978-1-912282-02-9 (e-book)

Notice
The information in this book is designed to orientate readers of the work under analysis,
to elucidate and contextualise its key ideas and themes, and to aid in the development
of critical thinking skills. It is not meant to be used, nor should it be used, as a
substitute for original thinking or in place of original writing or research. References and
notes are provided for informational purposes and their presence does not constitute
endorsement of the information or opinions therein. This book is presented solely for
educational purposes. It is sold on the understanding that the publisher is not engaged
to provide any scholarly advice. The publisher has made every effort to ensure that
this book is accurate and up-to-date, but makes no warranties or representations with
regard to the completeness or reliability of the information it contains. The information
and the opinions provided herein are not guaranteed or warranted to produce particular
results and may not be suitable for students of every ability. The publisher shall not be
liable for any loss, damage or disruption arising from any errors or omissions, or from
the use of this book, including, but not limited to, special, incidental, consequential or
other damages caused, or alleged to have been caused, directly or indirectly, by the
information contained within.

CONTENTS

THE MACAT LIBRARY

The Macat Library is a series of unique academic explorations of seminal works in the humanities and social sciences – books and papers that have had a significant and widely recognised impact on their disciplines. It has been created to serve as much more than just a summary of what lies between the covers of a great book. It illuminates and explores the influences on, ideas of, and impact of that book. Our goal is to offer a learning resource that encourages critical thinking and fosters a better, deeper understanding of important ideas.

Each publication is divided into three Sections: Influences, Ideas, and Impact. Each Section has four Modules. These explore every important facet of the work, and the responses to it.

This Section-Module structure makes a Macat Library book easy to use, but it has another important feature. Because each Macat book is written to the same format, it is possible (and encouraged!) to cross-reference multiple Macat books along the same lines of inquiry or research. This allows the reader to open up interesting interdisciplinary pathways.

To further aid your reading, lists of glossary terms and people mentioned are included at the end of this book (these are indicated by an asterisk [*] throughout) – as well as a list of works cited.

Macat has worked with the University of Cambridge to identify the elements of critical thinking and understand the ways in which six different skills combine to enable effective thinking.
Three allow us to fully understand a problem; three more give us the tools to solve it. Together, these six skills make up the **PACIER** model of critical thinking. They are:

ANALYSIS – understanding how an argument is built
EVALUATION – exploring the strengths and weaknesses of an argument
INTERPRETATION – understanding issues of meaning

CREATIVE THINKING – coming up with new ideas and fresh connections
PROBLEM-SOLVING – producing strong solutions
REASONING – creating strong arguments

To find out more, visit **WWW.MACAT.COM.**

CRITICAL THINKING AND *ETHICS*

Primary critical thinking skill: REASONING
Secondary critical thinking skill: INTERPRETATION

Baruch Spinoza's *Ethics* is a dense masterpiece of sustained argumentative reasoning. It earned its place as one of the most important and influential books in Western philosophy by virtue of its uncompromisingly direct arguments about the nature of God, the universe, free will, and human morals.

Though it remains one of the densest and most challenging texts in the entire canon of Western philosophy, *Ethics* is also famous for Spinoza's unique approach to ordering and constructing its arguments. As its full title – *Ethics, Demonstrated in Geometrical Order* – suggests, Spinoza decided to use the rigorous format of mathematical-style propositions to lay out his arguments, just as the Ancient Greek mathematician Euclid had used geometrical propositions to lay out the basic rules of geometry.

In choosing such a systematic method, Spinoza's masterwork shows the crucial aspects of good reasoning skills being employed at the highest level. The key use of reasoning is the production of an argument that is well-organised, supports its conclusions and proceeds logically towards its end. Just as a mathematician might demonstrate a geometrical proof, Spinoza sought to lay out a comprehensive philosophy for human existence – an attempt that has influenced generations of philosophers since.

ABOUT THE AUTHOR OF THE ORIGINAL WORK

Baruch Spinoza was born in 1632 into Amsterdam's Marrano community of Jews who had fled persecution in Portugal. In 1656, the community excommunicated him for "horrible heresies"— apparently due to his unorthodox views on God and religion. Spinoza retreated to a small Dutch town where he worked as a glass lens-grinder. However, he continued writing, signing most of his works as Benedictus, the Latin version of his Hebrew first name. Spinoza was widely denounced as an atheist and heretic by both Jewish and Christian religious authorities, but a century later scholars began to take note of his work and he gradually came to be seen as one of the most original and important of all Western philosophers. Spinoza died in 1677, aged just 44.

ABOUT THE AUTHORS OF THE ANALYSIS

Dr Gary Slater holds a DPhil in theology and religion from the University of Oxford. He is currently a faculty member at St Edwards University, Texas.

Andreas Vrahimis is the author of *Encounters between Analytic and Continental Philosophy* (2013). He teaches at the University of Cyprus.

ABOUT MACAT

GREAT WORKS FOR CRITICAL THINKING

Macat is focused on making the ideas of the world's great thinkers accessible and comprehensible to everybody, everywhere, in ways that promote the development of enhanced critical thinking skills.

It works with leading academics from the world's top universities to produce new analyses that focus on the ideas and the impact of the most influential works ever written across a wide variety of academic disciplines. Each of the works that sit at the heart of its growing library is an enduring example of great thinking. But by setting them in context – and looking at the influences that shaped their authors, as well as the responses they provoked – Macat encourages readers to look at these classics and game-changers with fresh eyes. Readers learn to think, engage and challenge their ideas, rather than simply accepting them.

'Macat offers an amazing first-of-its-kind tool for interdisciplinary learning and research. Its focus on works that transformed their disciplines and its rigorous approach, drawing on the world's leading experts and educational institutions, opens up a world-class education to anyone.'

Andreas Schleicher
Director for Education and Skills, Organisation for Economic Co-operation and Development

'Macat is taking on some of the major challenges in university education … They have drawn together a strong team of active academics who are producing teaching materials that are novel in the breadth of their approach.'

Prof Lord Broers,
former Vice-Chancellor of the University of Cambridge

'The Macat vision is exceptionally exciting. It focuses upon new modes of learning which analyse and explain seminal texts which have profoundly influenced world thinking and so social and economic development. It promotes the kind of critical thinking which is essential for any society and economy.
This is the learning of the future.'

Rt Hon Charles Clarke, former UK Secretary of State for Education

'The Macat analyses provide immediate access to the critical conversation surrounding the books that have shaped their respective discipline, which will make them an invaluable resource to all of those, students and teachers, working in the field.'

Professor William Tronzo, University of California at San Diego

WAYS IN TO THE TEXT

KEY POINTS

- Baruch Spinoza (1632–77), later known as Benedictus de Spinoza, was a Dutch philosopher. His *Ethics* was so radical that he was excommunicated* from his Jewish community, but the book is today considered a key work of modern philosophy.

- *Ethics* argues that everything is ultimately an expression of a single substance, which Spinoza calls God or, what is the same, nature. He rejects the common idea of an anthropomorphic* God (one who possesses human qualities, and who can love or punish people).

- *Ethics* shows that it is possible to think about how to live well in a world that has no purpose or pride of place for human beings.

Who Was Spinoza?

Baruch Spinoza was born in Amsterdam in 1632. His family were Marranos,* Jews who had fled Portugal after being persecuted. He received his education in the Marrano community of Amsterdam. The same community excommunicated him in 1656, apparently due to his controversial theological views. He went on to live in relative isolation, working as a lens-grinder in the small town of Rijnsburg and later in Voorburg and the Hague.

Following his excommunication, Spinoza took the Latinized form, Benedictus, of his Jewish name (Baruch), and wrote most of his philosophical texts using the new name. A particularly notable exception to this is the most controversial work published during his lifetime, *Theologico-Political Treatise*, an anonymous publication from 1670. The Synod,* or governing council, of the Dutch Reformed Church banned the work in 1674, by which time it was clear that Spinoza was its author.

Published after Spinoza's death, *Ethics* was almost universally condemned upon its publication. For a long time, philosophers would try to avoid association with Spinoza's radical ideas. It wasn't until a century or so after his death that his work began to be seen in a positive light in the context of philosophical debates.

Spinoza's bad reputation was, to some extent, the result of his own steady devotion to principles that went against the grain of the times in which he lived. Some of the things he fought for during his lifetime are commonly taken for granted in today's Western world, however, including his defense of religious tolerance and basic civil liberties.

What Does *Ethics* Say?

The emergence of modern science in the late Renaissance* led to the discovery that the earth is not at the center of the universe. This called for a radical reevaluation of our understanding of humanity's place in the cosmos. Spinoza's *Ethics* offers a guide to living in a universe in which human beings are bound by the deterministic* laws of nature—in other words, just as the natural world is governed by strict laws of science, the human world is regulated by laws that people cannot overturn through their supposed free will. Spinoza passes through various stages in order to finally reach his answer to the question of how to live well in a deterministic universe. The overall approach of *Ethics* is based on the geometrical method* first developed by the ancient Greek mathematician Euclid:* it begins with a series of definitions of Spinoza's terms coupled with a series of axioms* (self-evident claims), from which Spinoza seeks to demonstrate a number of proofs. His proofs cover a range of topics in philosophy and other disciplines, beginning with metaphysics* (the study of the nature of being) and theology, and moving on to epistemology* (the investigation of the nature and limits of knowledge), psychology, the theory of action (Spinoza's analysis of what it means to act), and finally an account of human freedom.

In his metaphysics, Spinoza develops a form of pantheist* monism,* according to which God is identical with nature. (Monism states that all existence is an expression of one single underlying entity; pantheism identifies that one entity as God.) He argues that the whole of reality is a manifestation of God, which he sees as the one entity underlying all of reality, and he uses the technical term "substance" to refer to this entity. Spinoza's God (or nature) is this one substance, which is not shaped in the image of man. God is not anthropomorphic (does not possess human qualities), and therefore God is not, as various religions hold, a being who is capable of loving humanity, or able to punish humans for their sins.

Extending his monism, Spinoza denies the existence of free will. He argues that human freedom involves a recognition that the world functions in a way that is deterministic (that is, every event follows from a cause that makes it necessary and inevitable). Based on this, *Ethics* offers an intriguing analysis of human emotions, which are seen as stemming from joy, sadness, and desire. These, in turn, he views as expressions of the effort to persist in being (the drive to survive and prosper). Spinoza argues that the blessed life lies in an intellectual love of God by people, despite the fact that God cannot love human beings in return. This intellectual love for God involves a knowledge and understanding of deterministic causation.*

Spinoza's thought was too radical for his contemporaries. His denial of free will and rejection of the anthropomorphic view of God were not ideas that seventeenth-century thinkers were ready to accept. Spinoza's thought became influential only after a debate over pantheism in late eighteenth-century German philosophy. This would later lead G. W. F. Hegel* to claim that, "You are either a Spinozist or not a philosopher at all."[1]

Why Does *Ethics* Matter?

Spinoza wrote *Ethics* in a manner that is often difficult to understand. Despite this, philosophy students who wish to follow the development of modern debates in metaphysics and epistemology are bound to read it. It contains, for instance, a significant and highly original discussion of the relationship between mind and body— which he sees as two distinct but parallel expressions of the same underlying substance. According to Spinoza's view, each event has parallel bodily and mental expressions.

Spinoza's work also contains some intriguing insights into the psychology of what we ordinarily think of as emotions, which he referred to as "affects." It offers a definition and in-depth discussion of love, hate, hope, fear, and other affects. Spinoza considers all these to derive from the three basic affects of joy, sadness, and desire. These are states of the body reflected in the mind. Furthermore, they are states that can take over the mind, preventing rational thought. Spinoza argues that having knowledge of the mechanisms at work behind such emotional states allows us to control them. This, in turn, is the foundation of living the good life. This view reflects the influence of the ancient Stoics* on Spinoza. The Stoics also considered the regulation of emotion as a pathway to the good life.

The above highlights the various levels of analysis at work in Spinoza's text. It begins with an abstract discussion of metaphysics and ends with a particular discussion of ethics. Between these comes philosophy of mind, epistemology, psychology, a theory of action, and a discussion of freedom. Various aspects of Spinoza's thinking have influenced people working in many different fields. From these lines of influence, many new strands of thinking may develop.

NOTES

1   Merold Westphal, "Hegel between Spinoza and Derrida," in *Hegel's History of Philosophy: New Interpretations*, ed. David Duquette (Albany: State of New York Press, 2003), 144.

SECTION 1
INFLUENCES

THE AUTHOR AND THE HISTORICAL CONTEXT

KEY POINTS

- Spinoza's book is a key text of modern philosophy. It addresses the question of how to live a good life in a deterministic* universe — one in which human action is not guided by free will.

- Spinoza was expelled from the Jewish community of Amsterdam for holding views that went against their established beliefs. He moved elsewhere in Holland and produced great works.

- Spinoza supported Dutch liberalism of the seventeenth century, which came to an abrupt end in 1672 when the liberal government was overthrown by royalist forces.

Why Read This Text?

Benedictus de Spinoza's *Ethics* is one of the most significant books in the history of philosophy. Written in Latin between 1661/2 and 1675 and published in 1677 following its author's death, the work owes its title to the fact that it addresses questions of right and wrong human action. Yet this title is misleading, as *Ethics* is also a book on God and the world, an examination of the structure of the mind and its relation to the body, a detailed account of the psychology of emotions, and an attempt to understand human action. *Ethics'* rejection of free will and exploration of the consequences of determinism—the philosophical view that all human action is determined by causes outside of free will—remains radical to this day. The book argues that altruism*—concern for the welfare of

> **❝** By the decree of the angels, and by the command of the holy men, we excommunicate, expel, curse and damn Baruch de Espinoza ... the Lord will blot out his name from under heaven ... But you who cleave unto the Lord God are all alive this day. We order that no one should communicate with him orally or in writing, or show him any favor, or stay with him under the same roof, or within four ells of him, or read anything composed or written by him. **❞**
>
> "Excommunication of Spinoza by the Talmud Torah congregation of Amsterdam," quoted in Steven Nadler, *Spinoza: A Life*

others—is a consequence of, rather than being contradictory to, the pursuit of self-interest. Its insightful analysis of human emotions concludes with an account of the good life as one characterized by joy and the power for action. The work is demanding for the reader, but is clearly a key text of modern philosophy.

The questions that *Ethics* addresses, including what the universe is, how we know it, how our emotions relate to it, and how we should act within it, are as important today as they were in Spinoza's time. It remains a lasting credit to *Ethics* that it addresses them in such a systematic and original way. Even the work's geometric style is not accidental. It reflects the author's belief in universal laws that govern everything equally and without preference or gaps.

Author's Life

Spinoza was born in Amsterdam, Holland, in 1632 and given the Hebrew name Baruch. Raised among that city's Marrano* community, he worked for a period in his family's importing business, while at the same time showing promise as a scholar.

Little is known about Spinoza during those early years, which seem to have involved a degree of controversy—most likely due to his controversial theological views. Such unorthodoxy was probably the reason why he was subjected to a knife attack in 1656.[1] On July 27 of that same year he was excommunicated* from his community in a writ of *cherem*,* the Hebrew term for expulsion of a member of the community. This followed accusations against him of "horrible heresies" and "monstrous actions."[2] The reasons remain unclear, but are likely to stem from his unorthodox views on prophecy, immortality, and God. Those who had lived, worked, and studied alongside him were then forbidden to associate with him. In 1661, Spinoza left Amsterdam for the village of Rijnsburg, near Leiden, in Holland, where he began work on *Ethics.* At the same time, he Latinized his name to Benedictus. In Rijnsburg, as well as across later moves to Voorburg and the Hague, Spinoza supported himself in his philosophical work by grinding lenses for optical instruments.

In exile, Spinoza corresponded with a network of friends and supporters who built his reputation and circulated early drafts of *Ethics,* at least across Holland and England. This group, many of whom were Mennonites,* members of non-conformist Protestant sects, attracted the suspicion of political and Church authorities. Those authorities grew increasingly hostile toward certain intellectual circles—if not wider culture—during the seventeenth century in Europe, particularly in England and the Netherlands. His friends encouraged him to publish *Ethics,* but Spinoza hesitated, discouraged by his excommunication and the hostile reaction to another work, his *Theological-Political Treatise,* published anonymously in 1670 and containing many similar ideas to those in *Ethics.*

Spinoza died from tuberculosis in February 1677. His death was possibly due to inhalation of glass, an effect of his work grinding lenses. *Ethics* was published later in the same year.

Author's Background

Spinoza's works were written and published during a turbulent period in the history of Holland. Political liberalism and religious tolerance played a central role in the Dutch Republic, which was headed by Jan de Witt* at the time Spinoza was writing. Spinoza was in fact granted a small pension by de Witt during the height of the latter's political career in the 1670s.[3] It was the general climate in the Netherlands, seemingly favorable to the circulation of liberal ideas, that made it possible to publish a number of controversial ideas put forward in Spinoza's works. Many of these are to be found in his *Theologico-Political Treatise* (*Tractatus Theologico-Politicus*, first published in 1670), which can be read as a defense of de Witt's political project. It should be noted, however, that even in this tolerant climate, Spinoza seems to have felt uneasy about publishing such controversial views in his own name.

Spinoza's caution would soon prove justified, as the fate of his work ended up being tied to that of de Witt's leadership. In 1672 (known in Dutch as the *Rampjaar* or Disaster-year), as a result of the Franco–Dutch War, de Witt and his followers were overthrown and lynched by royalists. Spinoza's anonymity was lost, and in this climate his work soon came under attack as being "forged in Hell by a renegade Jew and the Devil, and issued with the knowledge of Jan de Witt."[4] This led to it being condemned and banned by the Dutch Reformed Church in 1674.[5] *Ethics*, published after Spinoza's death, would come to be attacked in a similar way during the following century. This was a time when being described as a follower of Spinoza would amount to a kind of insult among philosophers. It was only around the late eighteenth century, and not without a measure of hesitation, that it became permissible to include Spinoza's work as part of serious philosophical debate.

NOTES

1   First reported by Pierre Bayle in his biography of Spinoza; see: H. M. Ravven and L. E. Goodman, *Jewish Themes in Spinoza's Philosophy* (New York: SUNY Press, 2012), 269.

2   Genevieve Lloyd, *Routledge Philosophy GuideBook to Spinoza and the Ethics* (London: Routledge, 1996), 1.

3   See: Roger Scruton, *Spinoza* (Oxford: Oxford University Press, 1986), 11.

4   Scruton, *Spinoza*, 11.

5   Scruton, *Spinoza*, 11.

MODULE 2
ACADEMIC CONTEXT

KEY POINTS

- Spinoza's thinking reflected the events of his time. Europe's religious wars led him to value the idea of tolerance, and the growing scientific revolution led him to question religious explanations about the world.

- René Descartes,* a leading influence on Spinoza, proposed that the mind and the body exist independently. Yet his theory of how they interact was considered inadequate by later philosophers.

- Spinoza rejected Aristotle's* notion of final cause. He also differed from Descartes in proposing that mind and body are two aspects of a single underlying substance (rather than two distinct substances).

The Work in its Context

Benedictus de Spinoza's *Ethics* was written during a period of change in European thought. Not long before, Europe had undergone the violence of the continent's post-Reformation* religious wars, and ideas of religious tolerance were forming in places such as the Netherlands, where Spinoza lived. The discoveries of modern science were, by now, in the process of replacing the old medieval scholastic* establishment associated with the Roman Catholic Church. The demise of scholasticism came with the collapse of a number of supposed certainties (the belief, for instance, that the earth is at the center of the universe).

Spinoza was affected both by the political developments of his day and by the questioning spirit of modern science. Having personally

> **&&** At last I have discovered it—thought; this alone is inseparable from me. I am, I exist—that is certain ... I am, then, in the strict sense only a thing that thinks; that is, I am a mind, or intelligence, or intellect, or reason—words whose meaning I have been ignorant of until now. But for all that I am a thing which is real and which truly exists. But what kind of a thing? As I have just said—a thinking thing. **&&**
>
> René Descartes, *Meditations on First Philosophy*

experienced religious persecution, he had come to see the priceless value of religious tolerance, for which he would argue throughout his life. Spinoza's view of religion was informed by the new types of questioning made possible by modern science, and by the discovery that the natural world can be explained through deterministic* laws of nature—laws that regulate which effects necessarily follow from which causes. A basic feature of Spinoza's thought is the embracing of determinism, accompanied by an attempt to examine how one may live a good life in a deterministic universe.

Overview of the Field

Spinoza and his contemporaries were writing at the start of a move away from the older Aristotelian philosophical tradition—a shift led by the rise of modern science. One of the movement's leading figures was René Descartes, who helped develop modern philosophy. Descartes argued for the separation of mind from matter. He called the material world *res extensa*, meaning "the extended thing," because he believed the property of spatial extension to be the main feature of matter. *Res extensa** exists separately from the realm of the mind (*res cogitans*,* the thinking thing). Mind and body are, according to Descartes, two distinct substances, and one can exist independently of the other. Descartes's argument allowed him to go on to claim, in his physics, that material objects can be explained on the basis of mechanistic laws. Material bodies are, according to Descartes, like cogs in a machine: the movement of one part of the machine inevitably causes the movement of another. The material world is governed by deterministic laws that can be discovered by physics.

The implication of Descartes's separation of mind and body is that whereas bodies can be accounted for by the laws of physics, minds are not governed by such deterministic laws. Thus minds, in contrast to bodies, can have free will. Descartes's account, however, faced a very serious problem from the start: given that minds and bodies are independent substances, how can the mind interact with the body? How is it that I can move a part of my body simply because I want to (that is, simply because my mind makes the free choice to do so)?

Descartes attempted to answer this question by proposing that a part of the body, located in the brain, interacts with the mind. This is not a satisfactory answer, however, since it relies on an exception to the separation of mind and body. Modern philosophers after Descartes, including Spinoza, sought to give alternative solutions to the so-called mind–body problem.

Academic Influences

Among Spinoza's main influences was his childhood education, which was shaped by the Jewish tradition and his exposure to philosophical figures such as the twelfth-century Jewish Bible scholar Maimonides* and the ancient Greek philosopher Aristotle. Beyond his home community, Spinoza studied Latin under Franciscus van den Enden,* a former Jesuit and political radical whose home attracted a circle of humanists and freethinkers, and to whom Spinoza's political views owe much.

In terms of the content of *Ethics*, it helps to distinguish pre-modern from modern influences. The impact of Maimonides can be seen in Spinoza's insights on the philosophical basis of law. Maimonides also helped shape Spinoza's argument that humankind is not the center of creation, as well as his identification of God as both the source of understanding and the totality of that which is understood. Another major pre-modern influence on *Ethics* was classical Stoicism.* The Stoics' claims that one ought to calmly accept what one cannot control shaped much of the latter three sections of Spinoza's work. Finally, Aristotle's philosophy provides the terms used in *Ethics* to address causation* and substance, even though the conclusions reached in both are radically different. Aristotle distinguished between two different types of causation. These he called efficient (what we would today consider a common-sense idea of one thing causing another; for instance, a boat's efficient cause is its builder) and final (a thing's purpose, for example, a boat's final cause is to sail on the water). Spinoza argued that the only true causes are efficient, denying the existence of final causes,* and thus putting forth a radical critique of teleology,* the study of the purposes of things. Moreover, while Aristotle saw the world as composed of many different substances, Spinoza argued that everything is merely an expression of a single substance: God or, what is the same thing, nature.

Among the work's modern influences, Descartes stands out. An established expert on Descartes, Spinoza employed Cartesian (that is, "from Descartes") terms in *Ethics* more than any other thinker. Yet as with Aristotle, Spinoza utilizes them to come to very different conclusions from those reached in their original context. Descartes presented God as substance in a unique sense, independent of all other beings in a way that applies to Him alone; he retained the world as a distinct realm governed by rational laws. Spinoza, on the other hand, transformed the idea of God into the concept of a unique substance, of which all other things are modes or expressions.

THE PROBLEM

KEY POINTS

- The rise of modern science made people question ideas to do with human beings' central position in the universe. Among these was the notion that people, in contrast to other beings, have free will.

- Spinoza worked at a time when modern scientists and philosophers, such as René Descartes,* were rallying against the more conservative scholasticism* of Europe's universities.

- For Spinoza, as for other rationalist* philosophers of his day, a key, unresolved issue, was how to explain the interaction between the mind and the body, which were understood to be two separate substances.

Core Question

The core question in Benedictus de Spinoza's *Ethics* is how to act in a universe that has no purpose or free will, or pride of place for humanity. The heart of Spinoza's answer to this question lies in one of the work's most original notions, that of *conatus,** Latin for "striving," which is the effort to persist in being (that is, to survive and prosper). Spinoza claims that to live a good life, one needs to act on the *conatus*, and follow one's self-interest.

Spinoza bases his ethical ideas on the claim that all human beings are self-interested, with each striving to persevere in his or her own being. For Spinoza, this self-interest is a virtue. It is important to note that, for him, the effort *to be* involves the exercise of the intellect (rather than, for example, a brute biological urge to struggle for survival).

> **❝** As far as good and evil are concerned, they also indicate nothing positive in things, considered in themselves, nor are they anything other than modes of thinking, or notions we form because we compare things to one another. For one and the same thing can, at the same time, be good, and bad, and also indifferent. For example, music is good for one who is melancholy, bad for one who is mourning, and neither good nor bad to one who is deaf. **❞**
> Benedictus de Spinoza, *Ethics*

As such, the *conatus* is closely linked with the effort to know or understand. Although this may seem like a license for pure selfishness, Spinoza intends it, conversely, to help explain how altruism is actually a product of the pursuit of self-interest. According to Spinoza, a self-interested person seeking the good life must be altruistic. In other words, there are good reasons for a self-interested person to care about the well-being of others.

Another effect of Spinoza's notion of *conatus* is that free will is an illusion, at least in the sense that one thinks of willful action as a power of the mind over the body. As he puts it, "In the mind there is no absolute, or free, will, but the mind is determined to will this or that by a cause which is also determined by another, and this again by another, and so to infinity."[1]

The Participants
At the time when Spinoza wrote *Ethics*, the key intellectual conflict was the struggle between scholastic* and modern thinkers over the fate of the European universities. Since the Middle Ages, intellectual life in the universities had been dominated by scholasticism, which favored lengthy debates over the logic and metaphysics* (which examines the

nature of being) of texts by Aristotle* and other authoritative writers. By the seventeenth century, greater interest in the investigation of nature, and horror at the continent's bloody experiences of religious conflict, had prompted a search for new methods through which to establish knowledge. Such attempts emphasized observation and experimentation, and styles of communication that sought to be universal—cutting across cultural differences. Along with René Descartes, who came before him, Spinoza allied himself firmly with the modern philosophers, and *Ethics* stands at the forefront of this intellectual shift. By the time Spinoza began to write, the modern Cartesian rationalist approach to philosophy had already started to be established as an alternative to scholasticism. Rationalism, in contrast to empiricism*—which held that all knowledge is acquired through observation—maintained that some knowledge is derived through reason alone. Apart from Descartes, who instigated this movement, leading representatives of rationalist philosophy included Nicolas Malebranche* and, at a later stage, Gottfried Wilhelm von Leibniz.*

The Contemporary Debate

Spinoza lived and worked at a time when the rise of modern science had led people to question Aristotle's scholasticism. One central Aristotelian concept under scrutiny was the notion of "final cause."* According to Aristotle, in order to fully understand a phenomenon under investigation, one needs to understand its purpose or final cause (in Greek, its *telos*), which is the answer to the question "what is it for?" Thus, an Aristotelian natural philosopher would consider an examination of purposes (teleology*) to be a crucial part of all science. Modern science would hold no place for teleological explanations. Descartes, for example, argued that material things can be fully explained on the basis of deterministic (or "mechanistic," as he called them) laws of nature, which require no reference to purpose for their explanation. Yet Descartes also argued that, apart from material things, there are also mental things, which are not subject to mechanistic laws.

Spinoza's metaphysics relies on his discussion of the concept of "substance," which he inherits directly from Descartes. Descartes in turn introduces it into modern philosophical discussions by radically revising earlier Aristotelian conceptions of substance. According to Descartes, a substance is a thing whose existence does not depend on the existence of any other thing. Descartes divides substances into two kinds: infinite and finite. There is only one infinite substance, according to Descartes, which goes under the name of God. God is self-caused and needs no other entity in order to exist. By contrast, a finite substance is one whose existence is dependent *only* on the existence of the infinite substance, God, who creates it. Once it is created by God, a finite substance's existence is independent of any other substance. There are two finite substances according to Descartes: mind and body. He argues that mind can exist even if there are no bodies, and vice versa.

This, in turn, gave rise to a debate among rationalist philosophers of the day over how these two distinct substances, mind and body, causally interact with each other. How, for example, can my wish to raise my arm be the cause of my raising my arm? Given Descartes's view that mind and body are separate, this is difficult to answer. He himself ventured that there is a part of the brain that somehow allows the mind to command the body. However, this seems to contradict his insistence on the separateness of mind and body—it appears to suggest the existence of a bodily thing that is mental. Some Cartesian philosophers had attempted to solve the problem by denying that there is any causal interaction between mind and body, a view that Spinoza also defended.

NOTES

1   Benedictus de Spinoza, *Ethics*, in *A Spinoza Reader: The Ethics and Other Works*, trans. Edwin Curley (Princeton: Princeton University Press, 1996), 146.

MODULE 4
THE AUTHOR'S CONTRIBUTION

KEY POINTS

- *Ethics* teaches that in order to live well in a universe with no place for free will, human beings need to understand our own psychological states and to discipline them.

- Spinoza felt the precision of his philosophy could best be expressed through Euclid's* geometry. He defined God as "the absolute infinite."

- Spinoza's *Ethics* is based on the rationalist* framework introduced by René Descartes.* But while Descartes's model allows people free will, Spinoza's determinism* does not.

Author's Aims

The fundamental aim of Benedictus de Spinoza's *Ethics* is to point the way to human well-being in a deterministic world that is indifferent to our concerns. The way to do this is by coming to a clear understanding of the causes of events, material and mental, and thus to reach the clearest possible comprehension of the world. An account of metaphysics* and epistemology* (the branches of philosophy that examine the concept of being, and the nature and limits of knowledge, respectively) serves as a foundation for Spinoza's psychology, which in turn leads to his theory of action and his overall account of how to live a good life. Thus the final aim of offering an account of the good life involves dealing with serious issues in the fields mentioned above. *Ethics* first tackles the most abstract questions, then moves systematically toward the particulars.

And so *Ethics* begins with a basic questioning of the nature of

> ❝ But I think I have shown clearly enough … that from God's supreme power, *or* infinite nature, infinitely many things in infinitely many modes, that is, all things, have necessarily flowed, or always follow, by the same necessity and in the same way as from the nature of a triangle it follows, from eternity and to eternity, that its three angles are equal to two right angles. ❞
>
> Benedictus de Spinoza, *Ethics*

substance. Here Spinoza intends to clear up several problems found in previous philosophers' accounts of the topic, particularly that of René Descartes, whose concept of substance led him to claim that mind and body are two completely distinct substances. This, in turn, raised the difficult question of how minds and bodies interact, with one causing an effect in the other. Spinoza seeks to overcome the issue by arguing that mind and body can have no causal interaction (one cannot bring about action or changes in the other). *Ethics* includes an intriguing reformulation of Descartes's problem, one consequence of which is that Spinoza embraces determinism.

Spinoza extends his redefinition of substance, and his response to Descartes's problem, into the realm of epistemology. He aims to offer a rationalist account of knowledge (in other words, to claim that knowledge acquired through the senses is somehow incomplete in comparison to the mind's knowledge of itself). This underpins Spinoza's psychology, which attempts to show how our mind's knowledge of the causes of our emotions is the basis for living the good life in a deterministic universe.

Approach
Spinoza placed a high value on disciplined philosophical expression, which he felt could be best achieved through mathematics. He

valued Euclid's geometry* as the ideal way to express philosophical ideas, and aimed to "consider human actions and appetites just as if it were a question of lines, planes, and bodies."[1] He does this by proceeding in his writing in the manner of geometrical texts, starting with a set of definitions of his terms. For example, he defines God as, "a being absolutely infinite, that is, a substance consisting of an infinity of attributes, of which each one expresses an eternal and infinite essence."[2] This definition was, in turn, based on previous definitions of "substance" and "attributes." Having defined his basic terms, Spinoza then goes on to offer axioms* (self-evident claims), such as, "Whatever is, is either in itself or in another."[3]

As in geometrical treatises, Spinoza's axioms are to be thought of as self-evident truths that cannot themselves be proven. The axioms and definitions are the basis on which all subsequent proofs will follow. All the remaining material consists of proofs, demonstrations, and *scholia**—explanatory comments on specific demonstrations and proofs. The proofs are demonstrated either purely by reference to the definitions and axioms, or by reference to previously established proofs. Thus, as the text proceeds, it builds on earlier material.

Contribution in Context

Though Spinoza presents his definitions and axioms as general and timeless, they often contain ideas that he would claim were specifically acceptable to the philosophers of his era. Thus, for example, his definition of terms such as "substance," "attribute," and "mode" rely on Descartes's use of these terms.[4] Spinoza adopts the vocabulary of Cartesian philosophy but revises some of its basic concepts in order to address some of the fundamental problems posed by Descartes. In particular, Spinoza uses the Cartesian definition of "substance" to argue that there is an inconsistency, or contradiction, in Descartes's own use of the term. Spinoza argues, first, that if one follows the Cartesian definition of substance,[5] there cannot be more than one substance with any given attribute and,[6] second, that a substance can be produced only by another substance of the same kind.[7] These claims have radical consequences. The boldest are that substances cannot be produced and are therefore eternal[8] and without purpose.[9] Moreover, God must be the only substance and consist of infinite attributes,[10] and everything else must be a mode—or expression in another form—of God.[11]

Though starting off with assumptions common among rationalist philosophers of his day, Spinoza reaches a view that is quite remote from their outlook. In particular, his conclusion that there can be only one substance undoes Descartes's attempt to save the notion of free will from the determinism that comes with modern science. Descartes thought that determinism applies only to the material substance (that is, matter always obeys the laws of physics), while the mental substance is free from the laws of physics. Spinoza shows that this is based on an inconsistent use of the concept of substance, which in Spinoza's system forms the basis for determinism. In other words, for Spinoza, there is no free will, since the mind too is subject to the laws of the universe.

NOTES

1   Benedictus de Spinoza, *Ethics*, in *A Spinoza Reader: The Ethics and Other Works*, trans. Edwin Curley (Princeton: Princeton University Press, 1996), 152.

2   Spinoza, *Ethics*, 85.

3   Spinoza, *Ethics*, 86.

4   René Descartes, *Principles of Philosophy*, trans. V. Rodger Miller and R. P. Miller (London: Reidel, 1983), part I, sections 51–6.

5   Spinoza, *Ethics*, 85.

6   Spinoza, *Ethics*, 87.

7   Spinoza, *Ethics*, 87.

8   Spinoza, *Ethics*, 88–90, 100.

9   Spinoza, *Ethics*, 97.

10   Spinoza, *Ethics*, 90.

11   Spinoza, *Ethics*, 94.

SECTION 2
IDEAS

MAIN IDEAS

KEY POINTS

- Spinoza differs from Descartes* in putting forward the idea of "substance monism,"* the belief that there exists only one "substance," which he identifies as "God or nature."

- *Ethics* opens with an examination of "substance." Spinoza presents a discussion of the two key categories that define substance: attribute and mode.

- The book uses a framework based on Euclidean* geometry,* whose cold rational precision reflects Spinoza's idea of a universe that is indifferent to human beings.

Key Themes

Benedictus de Spinoza's *Ethics* begins with a definition of some basic metaphysical terms such as "substance," "attribute," and "mode." Based on these definitions, Spinoza argues in favor of "substance monism," the notion that there can exist only one substance, which he identifies as "God or nature."[1] Spinoza seems to be claiming here that God and nature are one and the same "substance," a view that is called pantheism.* This one substance has two fundamental qualities, which, following Descartes, Spinoza identifies as mind and body. He further argues that these two qualities exist in parallel, and that every event is a mode (or different expression) of the one substance, and has both a mental and a bodily expression.

The text consists of five mutually reinforcing sections. It argues that human freedom lies in the exercise of the intellect, while clarifying the nature of knowing, the nature of being, and God. Given their centrality in *Ethics*' argument, these main metaphysical concepts are

> ❝ I shall consider human actions and appetites just as if it were a question of lines, planes, and bodies. ❞
>
> Benedictus de Spinoza, *Ethics*

fully developed in the book. The sections in *Ethics* on epistemology*
and theory of action are considered to be equally important.

Exploring the Ideas

Spinoza opens *Ethics* with an argument regarding the nature of
substance, which he defines, under the influence of Descartes, as
"what is in itself and conceived through itself."[2] In other words,
Spinoza holds that a "substance" is that kind of entity that can
exist independently of other entities (one whose existence is not
determined by, and does not presuppose, the existence of another
kind of entity).

Beginning with this definition, Spinoza draws a number of
conclusions about the nature of substance. He rejects the distinction
between what Descartes had called "finite substances," that is,
substances (*res cogitans** and *res extensa**) that exist independently
of each other, but are created by an "infinite substance" (Descartes's
God). According to Spinoza, there can be only one substance,
which he famously referred to as God or nature (*Deus sive Natura*).

As we have seen, Spinoza's system looks at the category of
substance. This is a crucial ontological* factor (that is, it relates to
the study of being). Spinoza also employs two other categories:
the "attributes" of the one substance and the "modes" of the one
substance. At the start of *Ethics*, he defines the category of attribute
as "what the intellect perceives of a substance, as constituting its
essence."[3] It is difficult to make out exactly what Spinoza means by
this unclear definition, which has been interpreted in conflicting
ways. As in the case of substance, he seems to build on Descartes's

concept of attribute, according to which the key attribute of mind is thought, while the key attribute of the body is extension—in other words, a body is, at its most basic, the kind of thing that is extended in physical space. Spinoza went against Descartes, however, when he argued that mind and body cannot be, as Descartes thought, separate substances; rather he maintained that mind and body are *attributes* of the one substance. For Spinoza, thought and extension are God's thought and God's extension (that is, they are essential attributes of the one substance, which is God). Somewhat confusingly, Spinoza seems to suggest that there are an infinite number of other ways in which substance manifests itself—human beings happen to have access only to these two.[4]

The third basic ontological category we find in Spinoza—along with substance and attribute—is that of mode. This he defined as "the affections of a substance, or that which is in another through which it is also conceived."[5] This definition raises the same problems of interpretation as those found in the definition of attribute, since according to this, modes are conceived through attributes. Any individual thought is a mode that can be classified under the general attribute of thought, and any individual body is a mode that belongs to the general attribute of extension. Infinite modes include the *general* laws governing all of thought, and the *general* principles governing all extended bodies (that is, the laws of geometry and physics). Finite modes, on the other hand, include all *particular* thoughts and bodies.

Spinoza's ontological scheme is the basis for his approach to Descartes's problem regarding the relation between mind and body. According to Spinoza, mind and body are simply two aspects of the same underlying reality, namely the one substance (God or nature). Mind and body are, Spinoza claims, two parallel ways in which this substance expresses itself: each event has a bodily and a mental aspect. For Spinoza, there is a mental event parallel to every bodily event, even if no human mind thinks it: all mental and bodily events are modes of the one substance (they occur in the mind and body of God or nature). Spinoza can thus go on to develop an account of human knowledge and action explained in terms of the relations held by human beings to the one substance's attributes of mind and body.

Language and Expression

Ethics unfolds within a framework explicitly borrowed from Euclidean geometry, which Spinoza valued for its precision, consistency, and universality. About 80 percent of the text of *Ethics* consists of an elaborate matrix of definitions and propositions that are self-referential—one definition or proposition often refers to others in the text. Yet each of the work's five chapters also includes textual passages, the so-called "*scholia*," which were written in a more accessible voice. Indeed, one senses in these passages a sort of detachment, irony, and even humor on Spinoza's part. This helps considerably to bring unity to many of the work's seemingly distinct projects. The question of the relationship between these two styles of expression—rigid mathematics and subtle irony— goes some distance toward making the content of *Ethics* as a whole more understandable. The claims of *Ethics* cannot be separated from the form in which they are presented. The eternal, changeless, and rational nature of geometric forms, which are indifferent to human purposes, supports Spinoza's view of the universe as purposeless.

Unfortunately for most readers, the mathematical style makes *Ethics* difficult to understand. Its vocabulary has been called strange, and its themes are extremely complicated, even impenetrable.[6] In spite of its difficulty, form and content combine in *Ethics* to generate a powerful set of conclusions for both public and academic life. All of this makes *Ethics* particularly useful when reading the history of philosophy as a source of cultural understanding in the present.

NOTES

1   Benedictus de Spinoza, *Ethics*, in *A Spinoza Reader: The Ethics and Other Works*, trans. Edwin Curley (Princeton: Princeton University Press, 1996), 97–100.

2   Spinoza, *Ethics*, 85.

3   Spinoza, *Ethics*, 85.

4   See: Abraham Wolf, "Spinoza's Conception of Attributes," in *Studies in Spinoza, Critical and Interpretive Essays*, ed. S. Paul Kashap (Berkeley, CA: University of California Press, 1972), 26.

5   Spinoza, *Ethics*, 85.

6   See: Beth Lord, *Spinoza Beyond Philosophy* (Edinburgh: Edinburgh University Press, 2012), 1.

MODULE 6
SECONDARY IDEAS

KEY POINTS

- Spinoza goes from some very abstract metaphysical* claims to some particular assertions on how one can live a good life. He does this by giving an account of the nature of knowledge and of the emotions.

- In his epistemology*, psychology, and theory of action, Spinoza demonstrates the implications of some of his most influential and perhaps controversial doctrines, such as his determinism.*

- While a lot of attention has been paid to Spinoza's metaphysics, his particular ideas about ethics have sometimes been overlooked.

Other Ideas

In *Ethics*, Benedictus de Spinoza's metaphysics (the branch of philosophy examining the nature of being) is intertwined with his epistemology (philosophical investigation into the nature of knowledge). The latter is largely an extension of his view of the parallelism between mind and body. Spinoza argues that the individual mind, rather than being a storehouse of private mental content separate from an outer world, is itself a part of the world that is closely bound up with the body; in a sense, they are two sides of the same coin. Knowledge is an essential part of the intellect. Spinoza here makes a distinction between knowledge acquired through the senses ("inadequate ideas") and knowledge acquired through either reason or intellectual intuition ("adequate ideas"). Our senses and imagination give us "confused and mutilated"[1] mental pictures of material things, which are partial

> **❝** By God I understand a being absolutely infinite, that is, a substance consisting of an infinity of attributes, of which each one expresses an eternal and infinite essence. **❞**
>
> Benedictus de Spinoza, *Ethics*

and subjective. In contrast, Spinoza claims that reason and intellectual intuition (*scientia intuitiva**) can lead us to knowledge of timeless truths. Here, Spinoza seems to be rejecting the empiricism*— which claims that all knowledge is acquired through the senses and denies the existence of knowledge acquired solely through reason or intellectual intuition—developed by his contemporary John Locke,*[2] with his emphasis on reason. Spinoza thus placed himself in the camp of the rationalists* (his relation with empiricism is, however, a matter of debate among scholars).

Spinoza's epistemology is applied to his psychology of the emotions, and to his theory of action. At the heart of these lies the *conatus** principle: "Each thing, as far as it can by its own power, strives to persevere in being."[3] Spinoza states this in the context of his discussion of the emotions, or "affects." He sees the affects as coming from joy, sadness, and desire—the three basic ways upon which the mind is acted. Joy is the result of an increase in the power to persevere in being, while sadness is the opposite; desire is the striving toward perseverance itself (that is, the effort to remain alive). All other affects are formed through combinations of these elements. For example, as Spinoza puts it, "Hope is an inconstant joy, born of the idea of a future or past thing whose outcome we to some extent doubt."[4]

Spinoza makes a distinction between passive and active affects. Joy and sadness are considered passive affects, as they are "inadequate ideas," or ways in which the mind is influenced by factors external to it. Joy and sadness can, however, be transformed into active affects once the mind grasps them clearly.[5] This means having an intellectual intuition of the affects as being the results of a causal chain that deterministically leads to them.

This takes us to Spinoza's theory of action, which relies on the argument that one acts rightly when aided by the intellect's recognition that free will is an illusion. Freedom, according to Spinoza, comes precisely from the realization that our actions are the results of a chain of cause and effect. In other words, freedom is not freedom of the will, which is illusory. Our language of good and evil has relied on a false conception of free will, which Spinoza's ethics revises on the basis of the *conatus* principle. The mind strives to persevere by turning affects from passive to active and understanding its own nature.

Exploring the Ideas

One of the basic ideas that takes us from the abstract metaphysical claims at the beginning of *Ethics* to its particular psychological and ethical claims is that of intellectual intuition (*scientia intuitiva**). Intellectual intuition is a third kind of knowledge beyond the distinction between reason and knowledge gained through the senses. Spinoza vaguely defines it as knowledge that "proceeds from an adequate idea of the formal essence of certain attributes of God to the adequate knowledge of the formal essence of things."[6] By intellectual intuition, Spinoza means grasping or intuiting that a thing follows necessarily from the nature of the one substance. This is neither knowledge acquired through reason nor through the senses, but is a third type of direct intuitive knowledge. In other words, it serves the crucial purpose of being the state of knowing in which the deterministic nature of the universe is glimpsed.

Spinoza's account of intellectual intuition relies on a crucial earlier step in his metaphysical system, that of distinguishing between *natura naturans** and *natura naturata*,* translated as "nature naturing" and "nature natured." This is a distinction between the "active" principle that produces nature, and its "passive" product. *Natura naturans* is the cause, while *natura naturata* is its necessary effect. Intellectual intuition functions as a means of granting the intellect direct knowledge of the whole of nature, albeit only as *natura naturata*. Intellectual intuition grasps the passive product, not the active cause of nature. It is a recognition that the specific thing under scrutiny follows necessarily from the nature of God—that it could not have been otherwise. Knowing things in this way is the basis of freedom from the bondage of passive affects.

Overlooked

Ironically for a work whose title is *Ethics*, it is the book's ethical content that is most overlooked. In the text's initially harsh reception, when Spinoza was charged with atheism* and his ideas were rejected across Europe, it was his views on God that received the most attention. Even a century after the book's publication, during the German pantheism controversy* of the 1780s, which opened up *Ethics* to broader critical attention, the claims on God and nature in parts one and two rather than the ethics in parts three through five stood at the center of the discussion.[7] The consequences of this focus were that Spinoza came to be read as a metaphysician arguing from a particular tradition: pantheism*[8]—a tradition that was unacceptable to the established religions. A more charitable interpretation, however, would see Spinoza as seeking to go beyond tradition entirely, directing his project toward understanding human freedom. Focusing on metaphysics as a particular tradition at the expense of the book's insights into ethics does not do the work justice. It hides the sense in which all of its parts are intended to guide the reader toward Spinoza's critical inquiry into how one can come to live the good life, which Spinoza sees as a life of blessedness.

NOTES

1   Benedictus de Spinoza, *Ethics*, in *A Spinoza Reader: The Ethics and Other Works*, trans. Edwin Curley (Princeton: Princeton University Press, 1996), 135.

2   See: Alexander Douglas, "Was Spinoza a Naturalist?" *Pacific Philosophical Quarterly* 96, no.1 (2015): 85.

3   Spinoza, *Ethics*, 159.

4   Spinoza, *Ethics*, 190.

5   Spinoza, *Ethics*, 247.

6   Spinoza, *Ethics*, 141.

7   See: Friedrich Heinrich Jacobi and Gérard Vallée, *The Spinoza Conversations Between Lessing and Jacobi: Text with Excerpts from the Ensuing Controversy* (University Press of America, 1988).

8   See: John Dewey, "The Pantheism of Spinoza," *The Journal of Speculative Philosophy* 16, no. 3 (1882): 249–57; F. C. S.J. Copleston, "Pantheism in Spinoza and the German Idealists," *Philosophy* 21, no.78 (1946): 42–56.

ACHIEVEMENT

KEY POINTS

- Spinoza's *Ethics* constructs an elaborate system of proofs in a geometrical style, creating a highly interconnected system. Elegant as it is, it has the disadvantage that if one proof or definition is rejected, the whole work unravels.

- *Ethics*, today considered one of the most important works of modern philosophy, has influenced other great writers. Yet when it was published, it was seen as denying the existence of God, a grave scandal in the seventeenth century.

- Despite the fact that the highly interconnected structure of *Ethics* seems to come undone if any of its parts is rejected, the work is highly innovative and contains keen observations about human life.

Assessing the Argument

Benedictus de Spinoza's grand task in *Ethics* is to start out from a number of abstract axioms* (self-evident claims) and definitions, and through a series of proofs present a thorough view of God, human knowledge, the psychology of affects, and freedom. The sheer breadth of this task can be intimidating to the reader, as can the precision with which Spinoza undertakes it. The text builds on itself, with each new proof relying on earlier definitions, axioms, and proofs. At times it feels like a maze: Spinoza continually refers back to earlier proofs, in the geometrical style that he adopts in his writing.

> ❝ You are either a Spinozist or not a philosopher at all. ❞
>
> G. W. F. Hegel, *Lectures on the History of Philosophy*

Spinoza's geometrical method creates a system with one big disadvantage: if one were to reject some evidence, axiom, or definition in *Ethics*, all of the other elements would have to be rejected as well. Due to its argumentative structure—the geometrical method—the text's grand systematic achievements can be dismissed by rejecting details, without paying careful attention to the entirety of its system, and there are many good reasons for rejecting a number of Spinoza's views. For example, his ambitious task includes an attempt to prove God's existence. Though proving God's existence was a key part of philosophy at the time, later developments in the history of philosophy raise questions about such efforts. Further doubts remain about the internal logic of Spinoza's arguments, since it is not clear that accepting all of his definitions and axioms leads to an acceptance of all his proofs. He sometimes relies on *scholia** or new definitions placed in the text to introduce views that could not be proven by earlier definitions or axioms.

Spinoza's conclusions are often more interesting than the formal reasoning through which they are obtained, and may merit reworking by contemporary philosophers.

Achievement in Context

Given the difficulties the book presents to the reader, it is possible to misunderstand its more controversial views, such as those regarding the nature of God. For a century or so after its publication, for example, the theology of *Ethics* was interpreted as being atheistic,* or denying the existence of God. Later interpreters, however, took it to be pantheistic,* proposing that God is everywhere (a belief that clashes with most monotheistic religions).

Spinoza's thoughts on religion were considered radical. This meant his views were seen as a kind of heresy* in philosophical circles: being accused of "Spinozism" was taken to be an insult against which one ought to defend oneself. Yet these attacks on Spinoza's thought came more from a cultural bias rather than from a balanced analysis of his philosophical arguments. The context in which he was writing would not have accepted as normal the idea that the word "God" might be followed by the phrase "or nature." Similarly, most philosophers would have been upset with Spinoza's arguments against anthropomorphic* conceptions of God.

Ethics remains one of the most important works of philosophy ever written. This is because of the range of concerns it deals with, covering everything from the nature of being to the mind's relationship to the body and the ways to achieve happiness in a deterministic* world. These topics go beyond philosophy itself, extending into cognitive therapy (a type of psychotherapy), environmentalism, politics, and art. For example, the Argentine author Jorge Luis Borges,* whose work blends literature, fantasy, and philosophy, claimed a considerable debt to Spinoza.[1] Likewise, Johann Wolfgang von Goethe,* one of the most famous German writers of the eighteenth and early nineteenth centuries, praised Spinoza for helping him calm his excessive passions as a young man.[2] In addition, Spinoza's work has been seen as bridging the distinction between Eastern and Western thought.

The style of *Ethics* is perhaps another reason why it is seen as so widely important. At the cost of ease of understanding, Spinoza deliberately selects terminology from mathematics as a means not only to express his points as precisely as possible, but also to communicate them in a way that is equally meaningful to all cultures. To be sure, Spinoza does not always succeed in this aim, and *Ethics* contains language that reflects the work's various historical influences. These include Spinoza's background in Marrano* Jewish thought, the Enlightenment* rationalism* of René Descartes,* and even the mathematical style itself, which is rooted in Euclid's* *Elements.*

Limitations

Spinoza borrows the style of Euclidean geometry*—for instance, the assumption that there is something intuitively obvious about the idea that two parallel lines extended to infinity will never cross. A similar case can be made about intuitively obvious logical principles, such as the principle of identity (A = A). No proof can be offered of this principle, though it can be thought to be self-evident for all rational beings. The question is whether there is any natural reason for the reader to accept Spinoza's basic assumptions. In contrast with the intuitive nature of the principles of logic or the axioms of geometry, it seems it might take some more work to accept Spinoza's complex and unclear starting points. This risks upsetting the balance between abstract definitions and relatively more concrete claims—which is the structure of each of the work's five sections.[3] For if the more concrete claims depend for their truth on their more abstract counterparts, then rejecting those abstract parts also means rejecting all that is concrete that follows from them. Additionally, if, on the other hand, the work's abstract claims depend in any way on their more concrete counterparts, then this undermines the geometrical method, which proceeds from the abstract to the concrete. Yet despite its shortcomings, *Ethics* made important innovations in philosophy and develops a strikingly original theory of being, one with detailed observations about human life.

NOTES

1   See: Marcelo Abadi, "Spinoza in Borges' Looking-Glass," *Studia Spinozana: An International and Interdisciplinary Series* 5 (1989): 29–42.

2   Stuart Hampshire, *Spinoza* (Manchester: Manchester University Press, 1956), 18.

3   See: Guttorm Fløistad, "Spinoza's Theory of Knowledge," *Inquiry* 12, nos.1–4 (1969): 41–65.

MODULE 8
PLACE IN THE AUTHOR'S WORK

KEY POINTS

- Spinoza's earlier works, and his surviving correspondence with a number of people, provide insights into the development of his ideas.

- *Ethics* deals with many of the issues raised by Descartes* and his followers, such as the relation between mind and body. Spinoza's powerful writing played a big role in promoting the scholarly study of the Bible.

- Spinoza's excommunication,* and a biographical entry on him written shortly after his death, left him with a bad reputation for the next century.

Positioning

Ethics was Benedictus de Spinoza's greatest work. While he did write a number of other texts, these are of interest to us as much to gain further information about *Ethics* as for any insights they themselves contain. These other works show the development and the consistency of his thinking during the two decades between his excommunication and his death. The most notable among Spinoza's other writings are his letters to a network of people with whom he corresponded, his *Treatise on the Emendation of the Intellect* (1662), *Parts One and Two of the Principles of Philosophy of René Descartes Demonstrated According to the Geometric Method* (1663), the *Theological-Political Treatise* (1670), and his unfinished *Political Treatise*. It is helpful to take these in turn.

Approximately 50 of Spinoza's personal letters remain today.[1] These date from approximately 1660 through to Spinoza's death in

> **❝** The *Ethics* is not only Spinoza's masterwork, it is also his life's work. We know from the correspondence that he began writing it early in the 1660s, that a substantial draft of the work was in existence by 1665, and that he then put it aside to write his *Theological-Political Treatise*, which appeared in 1670. He had published his exposition of Descartes' philosophy to pave the way for his *Ethics* ... the *Theological-Political Treatise* had a similar motivation. **❞**
>
> Edwin Curley, "Spinoza's Life and Philosophy"

1677, and aside from what they show about the author's personality and character these are of interest because they reveal that as early as 1660, he was thinking deeply about several key claims, such as the unity of God and reason, that would later appear in *Ethics*.

Also significant among Spinoza's early writings, the *Treatise on the Emendation of the Intellect* ("emendation" means "revising" or "correcting") was begun in the late 1650s and addressed the proper means to achieving true understanding.[2] Like the letters, this work seeks to distinguish clear and distinct true ideas from the inadequate ones that mislead us. The text shows Spinoza's notable debt to René Descartes. Descartes's influence on Spinoza is most on display in the latter's 1663 text, *Parts One and Two of the Principles of Philosophy of René Descartes Demonstrated According to the Geometric Method.*[3] Written at the request of friends who wished to gain a better understanding of Descartes's ideas, this work is significant because it marked a turn toward the geometric style of *Ethics*. It was also the only text that Spinoza published under his own name.

The work that comes closest to *Ethics* chronologically was his

Theological-Political Treatise, published in 1670.[4] A sort of plain-language introduction to some of the ideas that *Ethics* would later express geometrically, the *Treatise* offers a rationalist basis for religious liberty, and was published during a break in composing *Ethics.*

A final work, one that was never finished and remains a bit of a mystery, is the *Political Treatise.*[5] Spinoza began it in the middle of 1676, after *Ethics* had been completed. Intended as a sequel to the *Theological-Political Treatise,* it aimed to show how states with different constitutions can be made to function well, and thus serve as an argument for democracy. Despite the interest attracted by these other texts, Spinoza's reputation depends mainly on his main work, *Ethics.*

Integration

The whole of Spinoza's output might have seemed inconsistent if he had not published *Ethics.* The topics dealt with in his previous writings involved a clear interest in the philosophy of Descartes and his followers, which had, at the time Spinoza was writing, only shortly before come to dominate philosophical discussion in the Netherlands. On the other hand, Spinoza seems deeply concerned with theological and political issues, single-handedly prompting the secular study and interpretation of the Bible. These two interests are the subject of the two most significant works he published during his lifetime, the *Principles of Philosophy of René Descartes* and the *Theologico-Political Treatise.*

These two texts are, however, in some ways synthesized in *Ethics.* The *Principles,* for example, introduces Spinoza's geometrical method of writing about philosophy. It also forms the background of his mainly Cartesian concerns within *Ethics,* which is to a large extent a response to questions raised by Descartes and his followers, such as the relation between mind and body. *Treatise,* on the other hand, deals with themes investigated in *Ethics,* such as the rejection of anthropomorphic conceptions of God (that is, the notion of God as having human characteristics), the psychology of affect and its place in religion, and the notion of freedom.

Significance

Ethics brings Spinoza's previous concerns together in a systematic manner, using its geometrical style to attempt to demonstrate his views. The work covers many areas, ranging from metaphysics* and theology to epistemology* and psychology, all of which are interwoven.

Though *Ethics* was Spinoza's most important work, for the century following its publication, other factors shaped Spinoza's reputation as a thinker. The rumors surrounding Spinoza's life, especially Pierre Bayle's* biography of him in his *Historical and Critical Dictionary* (1697), helped to establish his bad reputation. Spinoza's excommunication early in his life, as well as the controversy surrounding the publication of the *Theologico-Political Treatise* and his association with republican leader Jan de Witt,* gave hostile interpreters the grounds on which to read *Ethics* as a defense of atheism.* This is an uncharitable interpretation of Spinoza, especially given that he seems to hold that the highest state of being is what he describes as an intellectual love of God ("*amor dei intellectualis*"). It was only around a century after Spinoza had died, in the so-called pantheism controversy* among German intellectuals, that his reputation was reconsidered. This involved the development of a new interpretation of *Ethics*, no longer seen as backing atheism, but rather as promoting a form of pantheism (God is nature). This view may be more charitable toward Spinoza, though contemporary interpreters of his thought are still debating whether we should see him as an atheist, pantheist, or panentheist* (who sees God as *in* all nature).[6]

NOTES

1   Benedictus de Spinoza, *The Correspondence of Spinoza* (New York: Russell & Russell, 1928).

2   Benedictus de Spinoza, "The Treatise on the Emendation of the Intellect," in *Ethics: With The Treatise on the Emendation of the Intellect and Selected Letters*, trans. Samuel Shirley (Indianapolis: Hackett Publishing, 1992), 233–62.

3   See: Benedictus de Spinoza, *The Principles of Cartesian Philosophy: With, Metaphysical Thoughts*, ed. Samuel Shirley (Indianapolis: Hackett Publishing, 1998).

4   Benedictus de Spinoza, *Theological-Political Treatise* (Cambridge: Cambridge University Press, 2007).

5   Benedictus de Spinoza, "Political Treatise," in *A Theologico-Political Treatise and A Political Treatise*, ed. Francesco Cordasco (New York: Courier Corporation, 2013), 267–388.

6   See: Genevieve Lloyd, *Routledge Philosophy GuideBook to Spinoza and the* Ethics (London: Routledge, 1996), 40.

SECTION 3
IMPACT

MODULE 9
THE FIRST RESPONSES

KEY POINTS

- *Ethics* was at first blindly condemned for its supposed atheism* and immorality. It took a century before philosophers began to see a wealth of wisdom in the work.

- So strong was the condemnation of Spinoza that the famous philosopher Leibniz* joined in publically—even though secretly, he was in contact with Spinoza and adopted some of his ideas.

- During the pantheism controversy,* a hundred years after Spinoza's death, the leading philosopher Gotthold Lessing* admitted that Spinoza's pantheism* had influenced him, setting the stage for an acceptance of Spinoza's work.

Criticism

In the period following its publication, the reaction to Benedictus de Spinoza's *Ethics* was hostile, thanks in large part to accusations of atheism and immorality in Pierre Bayle's* widely read *Historical and Critical Dictionary* (1695). According to the intellectual historian Peter Gay,* Bayle's dictionary "misled a whole century."[1]

The first significant thaw in Spinoza's reception came in Germany in the 1780s, arising out of a debate between Gotthold Lessing and Friedrich Heinrich Jacobi,* which came to be known as the pantheism controversy. In search of an alternative to the forms of thought then dominant in the German Enlightenment,* Lessing had confessed to finding in Spinoza's *Ethics* a system he could embrace. Although the response to Lessing's admission was

> **❝** He asserts therefore the most infamous and most monstrous extravagances that can be conceived, and much more ridiculous than the poets concerning the gods of paganism. I am surprised either that he did not see them, or if he did, that he was so opinionated as to hold on to his principle. A man of good sense would prefer to break the ground with his teeth and his nails than to cultivate as shocking and absurd a hypothesis as this. **❞**
>
> Pierre Bayle, *Historical and Critical Dictionary*

not entirely favorable, the resulting discussion shifted significantly the way Spinoza was viewed. Rather than the atheist caricature of Bayle's *Dictionary*, Spinoza came to be read as the founder of his own coherent metaphysical*/ theological system: pantheism. From here, it was not long before philosophers across the German idealist* movement of the late eighteenth and early nineteenth centuries found parts of *Ethics* that appealed to them. Attention focused almost entirely on *Ethics*' metaphysics and theology (parts one and two) rather than its ethics (parts three through five). The leading German philosopher G. W. F. Hegel,* for example, argued in his *Lectures on the History of Philosophy* (1837) that Spinoza's idea of substance formed the "foundation of all true views," and that the real reason for the harsh reaction to his ideas was that the critics could not bear the thought of their own annihilation in the oneness of nature.[2] To a large extent, the pantheism debate was the start of patterns that continue to shape discussions about the place of *Ethics* in Western philosophy, from its being taken up on behalf of a variety of other agendas to the focus on the work's opening two sections—on God and nature—at the expense of its final three.

Responses

Since Spinoza died before *Ethics* was published, he never got the chance
to respond to critics of the work. Evidence from his letters, however,
suggests that he was often dismissive of even friendly criticism from his
peers.[3] Indeed, whenever Spinoza was confronted by someone with
whom he was corresponding over some difficulty in his work, he would
often brush the person off completely—a tendency that increased in his
later years. This tendency in Spinoza's letters leads to the suspicion that
his unflappable personality would have caused him to remain calm in
the face of criticisms of *Ethics*. Such self-control, at any rate, had been his
reaction to both his excommunication* and to the uproar surrounding
his 1670s *Theological-Political Treatise*, which among Spinoza's works is
the one that most resembles *Ethics* in content, if not in form. Of course,
this is speculation, as is the expectation that Spinoza's unfinished *Political
Treatise* would have contained responses to criticisms of *Ethics*. Given
the constant nature of his thought across his adult life, however, Spinoza
appears to have been very difficult to persuade.

One interesting incident in the history of philosophy in particular
can shed some light on Spinoza's response to criticism. The famous
scholar and philosopher Gottfried Wilhelm von Leibniz is usually seen
as a leading representative of the rationalist* tradition. That tradition
begins with René Descartes,* moves through Spinoza, and concludes
with Leibniz. Leibniz had engaged in correspondence with Spinoza,
and in 1676, after *Ethics* was completed but not yet published, even
visited him. Leibniz, however, kept this visit a secret, given Spinoza's bad
reputation. In the works that he published during his lifetime, Leibniz
was critical of Spinoza, and in particular he contrasted his own insistence
on the existence of free will with Spinoza's determinism.* He did,
however, seem to integrate a lot of Spinoza's ideas into his work, and
that published after his death seems to show that in private he also held
deterministic views like those of Spinoza.[4] This reflects the fate, within
the context of eighteenth-century philosophy, of ideas associated with

Spinoza.

Conflict and Consensus

Throughout the eighteenth century, philosophers overwhelmingly condemned Spinoza's work. Influenced in large part by the French philosopher Pierre Bayle's account of his life, Spinoza's work was hastily and unfairly seen as the work of an atheist, a man who had been condemned for heresy* by Amsterdam's synagogue, and whose *Theologico-Political Treatise* was banned by the Synod, or ruling council, of the Dutch Reformed Church. This meant that few scholars took a fair-minded view of Spinoza's work. One notable exception is to be found in Leibniz's private papers. These, however, would remain a secret throughout Leibniz's life; despite privately developing a deterministic world-view, Leibniz publically denounced Spinozist determinism, contrasting it to his metaphysics, which, he claimed, was a defense of free will.

Perhaps more than any thinker throughout the history of philosophy, Spinoza was radical enough that it took a century of scorn before his reputation began to be restored. His supposed atheism, combined with his radical, deterministic outlook, ensured that the widespread view among philosophers was of Spinozism as a kind of philosophical sin. It was only in the pantheism controversy, around a century after Spinoza's death, that a philosopher would dare to claim that Spinoza had influenced him.

NOTES

1   Peter Gay, *The Enlightenment: A Comprehensive Anthology* (New York: Simon and Schuster, 1973), 293.

2   Genevieve Lloyd, *Routledge Philosophy GuideBook to Spinoza and the Ethics* (London: Routledge, 1996), 16.

3   See: Benedictus de Spinoza, "Objections and Replies," in *A Spinoza Reader: The Ethics and Other Works*, trans. Edwin Curley (Princeton: Princeton University Press, 1996), 146.

4   See: Bertrand Russell, *History of Western Philosophy* (Oxon: Routledge,

MODULE 10
THE EVOLVING DEBATE

KEY POINTS

- More liberalizing attitudes in the nineteenth century helped turn philosophers' attitudes toward Spinoza from rejection to deep praise. Later, even great thinkers in other fields, such as Sigmund Freud* and Albert Einstein,* spoke of Spinoza's deep impact on them.

- Few scholars have become "orthodox" Spinozists in the sense of having adopted his whole project. But even today, the work of some scholars in various fields is sufficiently influenced by the philosopher that they can be termed Spinozists.

- Spinoza's *Ethics* is still being studied not only as a valuable contribution to modern metaphysics,* epistemology,* psychology, and ethics, but also as a text that can be linked to contemporary debates in philosophy of mind, radical political thought, ethology,* and psychoanalysis.

Uses and Problems

In the nearly three and a half centuries since Benedictus de Spinoza's *Ethics* was published, general hostility toward the work has given way to widespread admiration, a transition helped by the weakening consensus on religion, a liberalization of politics, and a shifting of philosophical interests. The near-universal rejection of Spinoza began to be overturned in Germany in the 1780s with the pantheism controversy,* which started with Gotthold Lessing's* admission to being a follower of Spinoza. The resulting debates gave

> **❝** Spinoza is the Christ of philosophers, and the greatest philosophers are hardly more than apostles who distance themselves from or draw near to this mystery. **❞**
>
> Gilles Deleuze and Felix Guattari, *What is Philosophy?*

rise to the first positive references to Spinoza. G. W. F. Hegel* went so far as to claim that reading Spinoza formed the starting point for all philosophy.[1]

According to Spinoza scholar Pierre-François Moreau,* the pantheism* debate marked the end of the Enlightenment,* helped to create the artistic and literary movement called Romanticism,* and brought respectability to Spinoza's thought.[2] Whatever the merits of Moreau's position, it is clear that ideas in philosophical circles had significantly shifted by the nineteenth century toward a more favorable reception of *Ethics*. For example, changing attitudes to atheism were such that Friedrich Nietzsche* saw in Spinoza a precursor. In the twentieth century, Sigmund Freud spoke of his high regard for Spinoza, and the twentieth-century philosopher Bertrand Russell* seems to have had a broadly speaking Spinozist view of ethics. Albert Einstein also thought highly of Spinoza. When pressed by a rabbi, Einstein claimed he believed in Spinoza's God, a deity that is rational and indifferent to human concerns. Interest in Spinoza is perhaps stronger now than it has ever been, and historical, textual, and philosophical work on him continues to appear at a rapid rate.

Schools of Thought

Several contemporary scholars work in a framework that can be considered Spinozist. Thinkers such as Edwin Curley* and Jonathan Bennett* have highlighted Spinoza's insights as sources for their own efforts to develop the philosophy of mind and to practice logical analysis with rigor and precision. Curley has presented Spinoza's analysis of the relation between thought and extension as properties of God,[3] and Bennett's *A Study of Spinoza's Ethics* draws many parallels with current debates in philosophy of mind and metaphysics.[4]

The twentieth-century French philosopher Gilles Deleuze* has combined cognitive therapy with radical politics to argue that reading Spinoza helps open the reader to new ways of thinking about current social and political issues.[5] Such insights have served to ground Deleuze's burgeoning discipline of ethology, which looks at human and social behavior from a biological point of view.

Akin to Deleuze's analysis, a small but growing strand of commentators maintain that one must understand Spinoza in a fuller and more complete historical context.[6] Robert S. Corrington* has applied Spinoza's ideas, particularly the distinction between *natura naturata** and *natura naturans,** toward what he calls "ecstatic naturalism." This combines Spinoza's naturalism with the German idealist* philosopher Friedrich Schelling's* emphasis on spontaneity within nature, as well as elements of the pragmatic philosophical tradition, to comment upon the experiences of the sacred within nature.[7] There are also Spinoza disciples who are not primarily philosophers, as was the case with Johann Wolfgang von Goethe,*[8] Jorge Luis Borges,*[9] and Sigmund Freud.[10] It is important to bear in mind, however, that among these figures, virtually none applies Spinoza's work as a whole to any project.

In Current Scholarship

Amid widespread agreement as to Spinoza's importance, there are nevertheless many different—even opposing—uses to which his thinking has been put. Deleuze,[11] for example, controversially reads Spinoza as putting forth a brand of "empiricism." In Deleuze's work, this stands as a rejection of the existence of transcendent entities, as found in Spinoza's identification of God with nature. For

Deleuze, Spinoza's understanding that the mind is equally subject to determinism* as the body has certain political connotations. It undoes the Cartesian insistence on the solitary nature of subjectivity, showing the mind to be a part of the world, involved in relations that determine its states. Deleuze's approach to Spinoza focuses on the practical implications of his philosophy, seeing Spinoza as integrating the theoretical discipline of ontology* with the practical discipline of ethics.

Many other current thinkers have instead focused only on *Ethics*' more theoretical aspects.[12] For example, there is an open debate concerning the relationship between logic and psychology in the text. Bennett has argued that Spinoza fails to properly distinguish logic and psychology,[13] whereas Albert Balz* argued that Spinoza's account of logic excludes psychology entirely.[14] Another ongoing discussion concerns Spinoza's concept of causality, upon which hinges the question of causality between mind and body. Charles Jarrett has claimed that *Ethics* argues that no mental event can cause a physical event, and vice versa.[15] However, commentators such as Donald Davidson and Olli Koistinen disagree.[16] These authors hold that Spinoza's denial of causal interaction can be countered through attention to what they call "transparent" causality, in which it is always true that if X causes Y and X is identical with Z, then Z causes Y. Thus, if a physical change in your brain causes a muscle in your arm to contract, and that brain change is a mental decision, then the decision causes your muscle contraction.

NOTES

1   See: G. W. F. Hegel, *Lectures on the History of Philosophy, Volume 3: Medieval and Modern Philosophy*, trans. E. S. Haldane and Frances H. Simson (Lincoln: University of Nebraska Press, 1995), section 2, chapters 1, A, 2.

2   Pierre-François Moreau, *Spinoza: L'expérience et l'éternité* (Paris: Presses Universitaires de France, 1994), 420–1.

3   Edwin Curley, *Spinoza's Metaphysics: An Essay in Interpretation* (Cambridge, MA: Harvard University Press, 1969).

4   Jonathan Bennett, *A Study of Spinoza's Ethics* (New York: Hackett, 1984).

5   Gilles Deleuze, *Expressionism in Philosophy: Spinoza* (Cambridge, MA: MIT Press, 1990).

6   See: Willi Goetschel, *Spinoza's Modernity: Mendelssohn, Lessing, and Heine* (Madison, WI: University of Wisconsin Press, 2004).

7   Robert S. Corrington, *Ecstatic Naturalism: Signs of the World* (Indianapolis: Indiana University Press, 1994).

8   Stuart Hampshire, *Spinoza* (Manchester: Manchester University Press, 1956), 18.

9   See: Marcelo Abadi, "Spinoza in Borges' Looking-Glass," *Studia Spinozana: An International and Interdisciplinary Series* 5 (1989): 29–42.

10 See: Walter Bernard, "Freud and Spinoza," *Psychiatry* 9, no. 2 (1946): 99–108.

11 Gilles Deleuze, *Expressionism in Philosophy: Spinoza* (Cambridge, MA, Mit Press, 1990); Gilles Deleuze, *Spinoza: Practical Philosophy*, trans. Robert Hurley (San Francisco: City Lights Books, 1988).

12 See, for instance: Jonathan Bennett, *A Study of Spinoza's* Ethics (New York: Hackett, 1984).

13 Bennett, *A Study*.

14 Albert G. A. Balz, *Idea and Essence in the Philosophies of Hobbes and Spinoza* (New York: Columbia University Press, 1918).

15 Charles E. Jarrett, *Spinoza: A Guide for the Perplexed* (New York: Continuum, 2007).

16 Donald Davidson, "Spinoza's Causal Theory of the Affects," in *Desire and Affect: Spinoza as Psychologist*, ed. Yirmiyahu Yovel (Leiden: Brill, 1999), 95–111; Olli Koistinen, "Causality, Intentionality, and Identity: Mind–Body Interaction," in *Ratio* 9, no.1 (1996): 23–38.

IMPACT AND INFLUENCE TODAY

KEY POINTS

- Since the pantheism controversy* of the 1780s made it acceptable for philosophers to discuss the rich contributions of *Ethics*, the book has inspired thinking in a wide range of disciplines.

- Spinoza's aim in *Ethics* was to discredit teleological* thinking (which examines the purpose of things), the belief in freedom of the will, and the idea of God as separate from the world. The work remains radical even today.

- Recent philosophical responses to Spinoza have focused not only on his metaphysics* and philosophy of mind, but also on his politics, and even his ecological thinking.

Position

Benedictus de Spinoza's *Ethics* has remained relevant since it was first published. Spinoza's importance has grown as the concerns of philosophers have shifted in the past three centuries toward perspectives more receptive to his claims. This is so, for example, when modern science seeks to identify laws that produce regularities in nature that also apply to human beings. It is also the case in radical critiques of teleological thinking or of hierarchies in politics. In short, thinkers of many stripes have found in *Ethics* a valued source of inspiration.

Interest in the work has continued across different fields.[1] Some observers focus on the continuing relevance of Spinoza's attempts to wrestle with problems in metaphysics, logic, or the philosophy of mind.[2] Others have admired Spinoza for the political implications of

> **"** Some lovers of Spinoza may find this kind of
> inquiry, as pursued by Bennett, offensive. He does not
> give Spinoza high marks for deductive rigor ... But
> we would do no honor to Spinoza's memory if we
> did not recognize that Bennett is approaching Spinoza
> in the spirit in which he would have wished to be
> approached. Spinoza would have had no patience
> with anyone who rejected the propriety of the kind
> of logical questions Bennett raises. **"**
>
> Edwin Curley, "On Bennett's Spinoza: The Issue of Teleology"

his thinking, his efforts to trace the limits of thought, or the positive impact his thinking has had on ecology—removing as it does any special status for human beings within nature.[3]

Changes in religious belief are also responsible for the rise in Spinoza's fortunes. The reception of *Ethics* was plagued by charges of atheism* for nearly a century after its publication—a period in which expressing atheist beliefs could amount to a death sentence. However, there was a clear change in the response to the work after the debate over pantheism* among German thinkers in the 1780s widened the range of acceptable responses to Spinoza's thought. By the later nineteenth century, such an anti-clerical (opposed to the power of priests) figure as Friedrich Nietzsche* could openly embrace Spinoza as an inspiration in denying free will, or in overcoming the dichotomy between good and evil as existing within the nature of being. References to Spinoza abound throughout Nietzsche's oeuvre, and range from him enthusiastically embracing Spinoza as his precursor to more critical remarks.[4] Likewise, Spinoza's support for naturalism* (which sees the laws of nature as governing the universe) have come to be seen as pioneering for many in the modern scientific community who consider themselves naturalists.[5]

Interaction

Mild-mannered in character, Spinoza nevertheless found himself at the center of controversy at many points in his life. Most notable was his excommunication* from Amsterdam's Marrano* Jewish community at the age of 24 as a result of the radicalism of his ideas and his refusal to compromise what he saw as the philosopher's duty to seek rational explanations. Thus, *Ethics*, while not written expressly as a counterattack, nonetheless presented a radical, direct, conscious challenge to many forms of established thought. With the aim of discrediting all forms of teleological thinking (seeing a purpose in the cause of all things), as well as the belief in freedom of the will, and in God as being separate from the world, *Ethics* was radical in its time and remains so today. Indeed, Spinoza's democratic impulse challenges the traditional idea of order and hierarchy to its core. Spinoza has been seen as a very early proponent of environmentalism.[6]

Ethics presents a way of doing philosophy that interacts with other disciplines, (for example, psychology and politics). Yet it cannot be reduced in its methods to any particular style other than the geometrical method.* In other words, form is essential to the content of the work, part of what makes it so unique and lasting, even if it is often confusing for the reader.

One of the most significant legacies of *Ethics*, one highlighted by such figures as Jonathan Bennett,* is that the work's failures are instructive, and at least force one to respond to the failures to provide a better alternative.[7]

The Continuing Debate

Much of *Ethics*' legacy lies in the fact that it makes an innovative case for the rules that govern nature and God alike to be eternal. Thanks to its complexity and range of applications, this argument has inspired a wide set of projects. Many of these projects have of course had their critics. Yet regarding *Ethics* itself, there simply are not many thinkers today whose primary aim is to criticize Spinoza. This is not to say that Spinoza's ideas are currently beyond reproach, much less that *Ethics* is no longer of interest. The philosopher of religion Martijn Buijs, for instance, argued recently in his paper "How to Make a Living God" that Spinoza's account of freedom suffers from its refusal to acknowledge the element of chance. In this respect, Spinoza is often compared unfavorably to the more open metaphysics of the German idealist* philosopher Friedrich Schelling,*[8] who wrote a century and a half after Spinoza, in the first half of the nineteenth century. The point, though, is that Spinoza's thought has been absorbed widely and deeply into the modern philosophical landscape. As such, most of the contemporary approaches to his work mentioned so far harness the innovations of *Ethics* rather than challenging it wholesale. Or, to put it another way, the text is simply so unique that criticisms rarely target it directly.

To the extent that one would criticize *Ethics*, there are several possible motivations. The most direct would be to tackle the work's theological stance, which goes against anyone who would argue on behalf of the separation of God from the world, or on behalf of a purpose to the universe, since the book attacks both those ideas.[9] Another critique could be made based on a pragmatist* approach, which seeks to justify philosophical claims by observing the practical results of their application. Spinoza's system would appear to clash with pragmatism, since his approach is completely self-referential and its eternal laws allow no gaps or possibilities for change concerning either nature or humanity.

NOTES

1   Benedict XVI, *Caritas in Veritate*, sec. 34, in Angela C. Miceli, "Alternative Foundations: A Dialogue with Modernity and the Papacy of Benedict XVI," *Perspectives on Political Science* 41, no. 1 (2012): 27.

2   Joshua J. McElwee, "Pope Francis: I would love a church that is poor," *National Catholic Reporter*, March 16, 2013, accessed on May 30, 2013, http://ncronline.org/blogs/pope-francis-i-would-love-church-poor.

3   McElwee, "Pope Francis."

4   See, for instance, Miceli, "Alternative Foundations."

5   Leonardo Boff, "Pope Benedict XVI is Leading the Church Astray," *International Press Service*, September 13, 2007, accessed on September 26, 2013, http://www.ipsnews.net/2007/09/pope-benedict-xvi-is-leading-the-church-astray/.

6   Simon C. Kim, "Theology of Context as the Theological Method of Virgilio Elizondo and Gustavo Gutiérrez," PhD diss., Catholic University of America, 2011, 300–8.

7   See especially: Paul E. Sigmund, *Liberation Theology at the Crossroads: Democracy or Revolution?* (New York: Oxford University Press, 1990); and Frederick Sontag, "Political Violence and Liberation Theology," *Journal of the Evangelical Theological Society* 33, no. 1 (March 1990): 85–94.

8   Joseph A. Varacalli, "A Catholic Sociological Critique of Gustavo Gutiérrez's *A Theology of Liberation*: A Review Essay," *The Catholic Social Science Review* 1 (1996): 175.

9   Kim, "Theology of Context," 295.

WHERE NEXT?

KEY POINTS

- Spinoza's text remains the focus of intense attention, particularly in its application to two areas: scientific and religious naturalism,* and social and political theory.

- Insights from *Ethics* have been applied to widely varied fields, including political theory, psychoanalysis, cognitive science, and ethology* (an investigation into human and social behavior from a biological outlook).

- *Ethics* is a key text in the history of philosophy due to its explorations of pantheism,* monism,* and determinism,* as well as through its particular answer to the question of how to live a good life.

Potential

Benedictus de Spinoza's *Ethics* continues to attract intense attention, and there is little reason to doubt that such interest will fall off any time soon. How interest translates into influence is a different question, however. The answer depends on the parts of the work being analyzed, as well as the projects and purposes to which a given commentary contributes. As to where things go from here, two particularly compelling areas stand out. The first concerns explorations in scientific and religious naturalism and the second concerns social and political theory. For example, Spinoza's naturalism has been employed as a resource for contemporary philosophers of science,[1] some of whom admire its exclusion of God as an external agent acting on the world. At the same time, philosophers of religion, particularly Robert Corrington,*

> ❝Obscure though Spinoza's ideas may be, there is no doubt that he was deeply committed to elucidating our everyday experience. Spinoza's metaphysics and epistemology make way for a kind of anthropology: a philosophy of human nature and a theory of how human beings relate to one another. Spinoza gives us tools for understanding ourselves and strategies for living well, something that few philosophers since the Greeks have attempted to provide.❞
>
> Beth Lord, "Introduction," *Spinoza Beyond Philosophy*

argue that Spinoza's naturalism opens nature up to theological enquiry.[2] Regarding politics, the anti-hierarchical tone of *Ethics*, in both form and content, as well as its resistance to teleological* thinking of all kinds, has proved favorable to the efforts of various contemporary French thinkers to radically critique existing ways of thinking about social institutions and language.[3]

Future Directions

There have been various twists and turns in the history of the reception of *Ethics*, from its rejection as atheistic* to its reevaluation as a key philosophical work through the pantheism controversy.* Its insights relate to many fields, from metaphysics* and epistemology* to political theory, psychoanalysis, ethology, and more. In its various forms, Spinoza's influence has been unpredictable, and in this sense, an open mind is needed when talking of future directions in the study of *Ethics*.

One example of a recent and relatively unexpected use to which Spinoza's thought has been put is found in the work of the neuroscientist Antonio Damasio.* His research, in contrast to the mainstream in cognitive science (the study of the mind), finds a neuroscientific explanation for affects (or emotions). In a series of books that are to an extent popularizations of more rigorous scientific work, Damasio rejects the Cartesian* focus on cognition (thinking) in recent neuroscientific work,[4] advancing instead a Spinozist focus on affect.[5] Drawing directly from Spinoza's psychology, he undertakes a neurology of joy and sorrow (that is, examining the neurological basis of those emotions). Though Damasio's particular views have been subject to criticism and rejection from various sides (including philosophers),[6] the general project of a neuroscientific analysis of affect is one that will continue to flourish. Such a general project also relates to technological advances, for instance, the field of affective computing, which studies the simulation of affects by computers. Damasio may not have got his Spinoza altogether right,[7] but he has taken one step in rightly implicating him in debates about these matters.

Summary

As long as philosophers continue to argue about mind, being, knowledge, or ethics, Benedictus de Spinoza will be read. His arguments on the perennial problems of philosophy are certainly original, and have influenced enough scholars of equal fame to Spinoza himself to ensure that *Ethics* appears in future philosophy texts. The fact that vital movements in contemporary philosophy incorporate close readings of *Ethics* indicates that even the work's complex details are likely to be the subject of ongoing study.

Spinoza's life is also worthy of continued attention. At a time in which one could be imprisoned or killed for holding unorthodox views on politics and religion, he refused to compromise. He saw it as his duty to seek the truth and investigate nature and the achievement of human happiness. Having been dramatically expelled from the Marrano* community of his youth, he lived a relatively isolated life as a glass lens-grinder in the Dutch countryside rather than give up his radical views. Many of those who knew him personally—even if they disagreed with his opinions—testified to his even temperament and congenial personality.

Unique in its form, breadth, and the radicalism of its content, Spinoza's work takes a varied mix of classical, medieval, and contemporary influences and weaves them into an intact philosophical system complete with its own methodology. In it, Spinoza asks how we maximize well-being in a deterministic universe without free will, and with no pride of place for humanity. The claims of *Ethics* cannot be separated from the form in which they are presented, which is a complex and self-referential framework of definitions and propositions. Spinoza is seeking nothing less than a new way of looking at minds, bodies, nature, and God, transforming them all into a single substance that stands as one of the most radical approaches to be found in the Western tradition. Spinoza's God, rather than being an entity full of emotions, goals, plans, and free will to act on the world, has none of these; He exists, rather, as a single substance uniting the physical and mental realms and identical with the eternal laws that govern all things indifferently, human or otherwise.

NOTES

1   See: Marjorie G. Grene and Debra Nails (eds.), *Spinoza and the Sciences* (Dordrecht: Kluwer, 1986).

2   Robert S. Corrington, *Ecstatic Naturalism: Signs of the World* (Indianapolis: Indiana University Press, 1994).

3   See: Louis Althusser, *For Marx*, trans. Ben Brewster, (CITY: Verso, 1969), 78; Gilles Deleuze, *Spinoza: Practical Philosophy*, trans. Robert Hurley (San Francisco: City Lights Books, 1988), 69–70.

4   Antonio R. Damasio, *Descartes' Error: Emotion, Reason, and the Human Brain* (New York: Harper Perennial, 1995).

5   Antonio Damasio, *Looking for Spinoza: Joy, Sorrow, and the Feeling Brain* (Orlando, FL: Harvest, 2003).

6   See: M. R. Bennett, and P. M. S. Hacker, *Philosophical Foundations of Neuroscience* (Malden, MA: Wiley-Blackwell, 2003).

7   Ian Hacking, "Minding the Brain," *The New York Review of Books*, June 24, 2004, http://www.nybooks.com/articles/archives/2004/jun/24/minding-the-brain/.

GLOSSARIES

GLOSSARY OF TERMS

Altruism: a concern for the well-being of others.

Anthropomorphism: attributing human characteristics to a non-human being (for instance, imagining that a car's lights are its eyes, or picturing a god as a large person).

Atheism: the denial of the existence of God.

Axiom: a self-evident assumption on which other deductions can be based.

Cartesian: derived from the Latinized version of the name of René Descartes (Cartesius), an adjective used to indicate ideas influenced by Descartes's work.

Causation: in philosophy, the study of the relationship between cause and effect.

Cherem: a Hebrew term for excommunication, a shunning or expulsion from the community of the faithful.

Conatus: in Spinoza's work, a term that stands for the force by which each thing strives to persevere in its being.

Determinism: the philosophical view that all events are determined by causes that could not have produced any other action. This involves the denial of the existence of free will, since determinists hold that human action is determined in the same way as all other action.

Empiricism: a strand of philosophy that emphasizes sensory experience, such as seeing or hearing, as the primary—perhaps the only—source of knowledge. It also refers to knowledge gained through observation and experimentation.

Enlightenment: an intellectual movement, primarily during the eighteenth century, that championed reason, challenged traditional political authority, and called for the spreading of knowledge among the population. Spinoza is often seen as an early promoter of radical enlightenment.

Epistemology: an area of philosophy that addresses questions relating to the nature and limits of knowledge.

Ethology: the study of human behavior and social organization from a biological perspective.

Excommunication: a shunning or expulsion from the community of the faithful.

Final cause: a type of cause discussed by Aristotle. He distinguishes, among other types of causes, between efficient and final causes. The notion of efficient cause is the current common-sense notion of cause: A is the cause of B if in some sense A preceded B in time, and B was its product or effect. Final causes (Greek, *teloi*), on the other hand, refer to what a thing is for, its purpose. For example, a boat's efficient cause might be the boat-maker who made it, while its final cause might be to sail in the sea.

Geometrical method: in Latin, *geometrico* (translated as "geometrical manner"), a particular method of proof found originally in Euclid's geometry, and applied by Spinoza to the writing of philosophy. It begins by offering definitions and axioms, and proceeds by developing proofs and demonstrating them.

German idealism: refers to a tradition in German philosophy that followed in the wake of Immanuel Kant's *Critique of Pure Reason*. Broadly put, thinkers within the tradition, which included such figures as G. W. F. Hegel and Friedrich Schelling, sought to investigate the conditions through which the mind interacts with the world.

Heresy: a deviation from the accepted theological views of a particular religion.

Marranos: Sephardic Jews in the Iberian Peninsula (Portugal and Spain) who had been ordered to convert to Christianity upon the defeat of the Muslim Moors in the region during the fifteenth century. Spinoza's family were Portuguese Marranos, formerly called "Espinosa," who had emigrated to Amsterdam in the 1590s.

Mennonites: a sect of Protestant Christianity, named after Menno Simons, that originated in the sixteenth century. Their rejection of infant baptism in favor of the baptism of adult "believers" brought scorn and persecution from other Christian communities, Catholic as well as Protestant. Mennonites are known for their pacifist beliefs.

Metaphysics: a term derived from ancient Greek philosophy, particularly that of Aristotle; it is the branch of philosophy that investigates the nature of being.

Monism: the philosophical position that claims that basically only one entity, or thing, exists. Substance monism is the view that only one substance exists.

Naturalism: a range of philosophical perspectives sharing the basic belief that natural laws are the basis on which all phenomena may be explained.

***Natura naturans* and *natura naturata*:** terms that translate from the original Latin respectively as "nature in the active sense" and "nature already created," or more accurately as "nature naturing" and "nature natured." This implies a relation of cause (*natura naturans*) and effect (*natura naturata*), or creator and creature.

Ontology: the part of philosophy that deals with questions regarding being—that is, what kinds of things, broadly speaking, are there, or exist, or what is reality made of?

Panentheism: the view that God is in everything that exists. It contrasts with pantheism in that pantheism holds that God *is* everything in the universe (God *is* nature), while panentheism holds that God is *in* everything in the universe (God is *in* all nature).

Pantheism: the belief that everything in the universe is identical with the divine. Although the term does not itself appear in the *Ethics*, the work is considered one of philosophy's most prominent pantheistic texts.

Pantheism controversy: this began in the 1780s as a debate between Gotthold Lessing and Friedrich Heinrich Jacobi in which the former admitted embracing Spinoza's philosophy, as an alternative to the modes of thinking then dominant. The debate raised questions that not only shifted the way in which Spinoza came to be viewed, but also marked a key transition in German thought from the Enlightenment of the eighteenth century to the Romanticism and idealism of the nineteenth.

Pragmatism: a philosophical tradition originating in the United States in the 1870s. Key figures include Charles S. Peirce, William James, and John Dewey, all of whom shared a commitment to observing and clarifying the effects of philosophical claims in lived experience.

Rationalism: a strand of Enlightenment thought that praised reason as both the means to access knowledge and indeed the repository of truth. Rationalism reached its height of influence in the late seventeenth and eighteenth centuries, and is contrasted with empiricism, knowledge gained through observation and experimentation.

Reformation: a process that began in 1517 when Martin Luther famously pinned his *Ninety-Five Theses* on the door of the church of Wittenberg, which would eventually lead to the Catholic Church's split from Protestantism.

Renaissance: a period in European history from the fourteenth until the seventeenth century, bridging the Middle Ages and modern history. It started in Italy as a cultural, intellectual, and artistic revival of ancient Greek culture. The word means literally "rebirth."

***Res cogitans* and *res extensa*:** Descartes's Latin terms for "thinking thing" (*res cogitans*) and "extended thing" (*res extensa*), meant to indicate the essential attributes of mind, which is characterized by thought, and body, which is characterized by extension in space.

Romanticism: a philosophical, artistic, and literary movement that arose in Europe at the end of the eighteenth century and beginning of the nineteenth. A reaction against the rationalist emphases on universality, reason, and mathematics, Romanticism emphasized historical particularity, emotion, and the spiritual qualities of the natural world.

Scholasticism: a philosophical approach that dominated within medieval European universities and was characterized by logical disputations, as a method of achieving the subtlest possible distinctions.

Scholia: the Greek word for "comments," used in the geometrical mode in which Spinoza writes to add less formal remarks.

Scientia intuitiva: a term that can be translated as "intellectual intuition," which, according to Spinoza, is a third kind of knowledge beyond that acquired through the senses or through pure reason.

Stoicism: a school of Greek philosophy founded by Zeno of Citium that praised control of one's passions as the highest good in life.

Synod: a church council or assembly, usually composed of senior members of the clergy.

Teleology: a term that derives from the Greek term *telos*, meaning "end" or "purpose," and which refers to both the study of purposes as well as any set of claims in which a purpose is implied as part of a thing or event's cause.

PEOPLE MENTIONED IN THE TEXT

Aristotle (384–322 B.C.E.) was a Greek philosopher who served as a pupil of Plato, founded the Lyceum in Athens, and composed treatises on almost every field of human knowledge, including ethics, aesthetics, metaphysics, and logic.

Albert Balz (1887–1957) was a contemporary American philosopher and historian of early modern philosophy.

Pierre Bayle (1647–1706) was a French philosopher who, following Descartes, advocated strict separation between faith and reason. His *Historical and Critical Dictionary*, first published in 1697, was widely read among European intellectuals at the turn of the eighteenth century.

Jonathan Bennett (b. 1930) is a contemporary British philosopher and historian of early modern philosophy.

Jorge Luis Borges (1899–1986) was an Argentinean writer and poet, one of the most important figures in twentieth-century literature.

Robert S. Corrington (b. 1950) is a contemporary American writer and philosopher.

Edwin Curley (b. 1937) is a contemporary American philosopher and Spinoza scholar.

Antonio Damasio (b. 1944) is a contemporary neuroscientist and author.

Gilles Deleuze (1925–95) was a contemporary French philosopher and historian of philosophy.

René Descartes (1596–1650) was a French mathematician and philosopher whose dualism between mind and world and whose philosophical method of clear and distinct ideas upon indubitable foundations marked the decisive turning point from medieval to modern philosophy, as well as a broader shift between philosophies of being toward those of consciousness.

Albert Einstein (1879–1955) was the most significant contributor to twentieth-century theoretical physics, known for developing the theory of relativity.

Franciscus van den Enden (1602–74) was most famous for having been Spinoza's teacher. He was, among other things, a political radical, poet, and philosopher. He spent a period of his life as a Jesuit, though he soon abandoned the order, and was thought by some to have been an atheist. He was convicted of having plotted to murder the French king Louis XIV and hanged outside the Bastille.

Euclid of Alexandria (c. mid-fourth century–mid-third century B.C.E.) was a Greek mathematician whose primary work, *Elements*, served as the textbook for math courses until the early twentieth century. He is considered the father of geometry.

Sigmund Freud (1856–1939) was an Austrian neurologist who is known as the father of psychoanalysis. In terms of intellectual history, Freud is significant, along with Karl Marx and Friedrich Nietzsche, for undermining the Enlightenment consensus that humans are fundamentally rational beings.

Peter Gay (1923–2015) was a contemporary American historian.

Johann Wolfgang von Goethe (1749–1832) was a German philosopher, writer, scientist, and statesman. He is known among other things for his association with the *Sturm und Drang* ("Storm and Drive") literary movement of the late eighteenth century.

Felix Guattari (1930–92) was a contemporary French psychotherapist, philosopher, and activist.

Georg Wilhelm Friedrich Hegel (1770–1831) was one of the most significant philosophers of the past two hundred years. Associated with the German idealist tradition initiated by Immanuel Kant, Hegel's brand of idealism, which he called absolute idealism, describes nature as an absolute system whose manifestations unfold across a logical historical path.

Friedrich Heinrich Jacobi (1743–1819) was a German post-Kantian philosopher and participant in the pantheism controversy.

Gottfried Wilhelm von Leibniz (1646–1716) was a German mathematician and philosopher who is credited, along with Isaac Newton, as an independent co-inventor of calculus.

Gotthold Lessing (1729–81) was a German philosopher and poet whose work marked a high point in German Enlightenment thinking before its transition into Romanticism.

John Locke (1632–1704) was an English philosopher and political theorist whose writings are considered foundational to empiricist philosophy and modern liberalism.

Maimonides (1135–1204), born Mosheh ben Maimon, was a twelfth-century philosopher and scholar of the Torah who lived in Spain and North Africa. Noted for his explications of Jewish law, Maimonides is also renowned for his synthesis of biblical and Aristotelian thought.

Nicolas Malebranche (1638–1715) was a Cartesian rationalist philosopher and priest. He is best known for his defense of a version of the doctrine known as occasionalism, which holds that mental events cannot cause bodily events, and vice versa; rather, each time the mind wills something, God causes bodily reality to make it so.

Pierre-François Moreau (b. 1948) is a contemporary French philosopher and historian of French philosophy.

Friedrich Nietzsche (1844–1900) was a German philosopher and cultural critic whose work radically challenged many of the most entrenched notions in Western thought, particularly regarding morality and religion.

Bertrand Russell (1872–1970) was a contemporary British philosopher and mathematician, and one of the twentieth century's leading public intellectuals.

Friedrich Schelling (1775–1854) was a German philosopher associated with the tradition of German idealism initiated by Immanuel Kant (1724–1804). He emphasized chance as an inescapable fact of nature.

Jan de Witt (1625–72) was a republican politician, first Statesman of the Dutch Republic from the 1650s until his death. He was forcibly deposed by royalists, who lynched him and his brother in 1672.

WORKS CITED

WORKS CITED

Abadi, Marcelo. "Spinoza in Borges' Looking-Glass." *Studia Spinozana: An International and Interdisciplinary Series* 5 (1989): 29–42.

Alexander, Douglas. "Was Spinoza a Naturalist?" *Pacific Philosophical Quarterly* 96, no. 1 (2015): 77–99.

Althusser, Louis. *For Marx*. Translated by Ben Brewster. New York: Verso, 1969.

Balz, Albert G. A. *Idea and Essence in the Philosophies of Hobbes and Spinoza*. New York: Columbia University Press, 1918.

Bennett, Jonathan. *A Study of Spinoza's Ethics*. New York: Hackett, 1984.

Bennett, M. R., and P. M. S. Hacker. *Philosophical Foundations of Neuroscience*. Malden, MA: Wiley-Blackwell, 2003.

Bernard, Walter. "Freud and Spinoza." *Psychiatry* 9, no. 2 (1946): 99–108.

Buijs, M. E. J. "How to Make a Living God" (not yet published).

Copleston, F. C. "Pantheism in Spinoza and the German Idealists." *Philosophy* 21, no. 78 (1946): 42–56.

Corrington, Robert S. *Ecstatic Naturalism: Signs of the World*. Indianapolis: Indiana University Press, 1994.

Curley, Edwin. *Spinoza's Metaphysics: An Essay in Interpretation*. Cambridge, MA: Harvard University Press, 1969.

Damasio, Antonio. *Descartes' Error: Emotion, Reason, and the Human Brain*. New York: Harper Perennial, 1995.

———. *Looking for Spinoza: Joy, Sorrow, and the Feeling Brain*. Orlando, FL: Harvest, 2003.

Davidson, Donald. "Spinoza's Causal Theory of the Affects." In *Desire and Affect: Spinoza as Psychologist*, ed. Yirmiyahu Yovel, 95–111. Leiden: Brill, 1999.

Deleuze, Gilles. *Expressionism in Philosophy: Spinoza*. Cambridge, MA: MIT Press, 1992.

———. *Spinoza: Practical Philosophy*. Translated by Robert Hurley. San Francisco: City Lights Books, 1988.

Descartes, René. *Principles of Philosophy.* Translated by V. Rodger Miller and R. P. Miller. London: Reidel, 1983.

Dewey, John. "The Pantheism of Spinoza." *The Journal of Speculative Philosophy* 16, no.3 (1882): 249–57.

Fløistad, Guttorm. "Spinoza's Theory of Knowledge." *Inquiry* 12, nos.1–4 (1969): 41–65.

Gay, Peter. *The Enlightenment: A Comprehensive Anthology*. New York: Simon and Schuster, 1973.

Goetschel, Willi. *Spinoza's Modernity: Mendelssohn, Lessing, and Heine.* Madison, WI: University of Wisconsin Press, 2004.

Grene, Marjorie G., and Debra Nails, eds. *Spinoza and the Sciences*. Dordrecht: Kluwer, 1986.

Hacking, Ian. "Minding the Brain." *The New York Review of Books*, June 24, 2004. Accessed September 24, 2015. http://www.nybooks.com/articles/archives/2004/jun/24/minding-the-brain/.

Hampshire, Stuart. *Spinoza*. Manchester: Manchester University Press, 1956.

Hegel, G. W. F. *Lectures on the History of Philosophy, Volume 3: Medieval and Modern Philosophy*. Translated by E. S. Haldane and Frances H. Simson. Lincoln: University of Nebraska Press, 1995.

Jacobi, Friedrich Heinrich, and Gérard Vallée. *The Spinoza Conversations Between Lessing and Jacobi: Text with Excerpts from the Ensuing Controversy*. University Press of America, 1988.

James, Susan. "When Does Truth Matter? Spinoza on the Relation Between Theology and Philosophy." *European Journal of Philosophy* 20, no.1 (2012): 91–108.

Jarrett, Charles E. *Spinoza: A Guide for the Perplexed*. New York: Continuum, 2007.

Koistinen, Olli. "Causality, Intentionality, and Identity: Mind–Body Interaction." *Ratio* 9 no.1 (1996): 23–38.

Lloyd, Genevieve. *Routledge Philosophy GuideBook to Spinoza and the* Ethics. London: Routledge, 1996.

— — —. "Spinoza's Environmental Ethics." *Inquiry* 23, no.3 (1980): 293–311.

Lord, B., ed. *Spinoza Beyond Philosophy*. Edinburgh: Edinburgh University Press, 2012.

Moreau, Pierre-François. *Spinoza: L'expérience et l'éternité*. Paris: Presses Universitaires de France, 1994.

Nietzsche, Friedrich Wilhelm. *Nietzsche: The Gay Science: With a Prelude in*

German Rhymes and an Appendix of Songs. Translated by Josefine Nauckhoff. London: Cambridge University Press, 2001.

———. *Selected Letters of Friedrich Nietzsche*. Edited and translated by Christopher Middleton. New York: Hackett Publishing, 1996.

Norris, Christofer. "Spinoza and the Conflict of Interpretations." In *Spinoza Now*, ed. Dimitris Vardoulakis, 3–38. Minnesota: University of Minnesota Press, 2011.

Peden, Knox. *Spinoza Contra Phenomenology: French Rationalism from Cavaillès to Deleuze*. California: Stanford University Press, 2014.

Ravven, H. M., and L. E. Goodman. *Jewish Themes in Spinoza's Philosophy*. New York: SUNY Press, 2012.

Russell, Bertrand. *History of Western Philosophy*. Oxon: Routledge, 2004.

Scruton, Roger. *Spinoza*. Oxford: Oxford University Press, 1986.

Spinoza, Baruch (Benedictus de). *The Correspondence of Spinoza*. New York, Russell & Russell, 1928.

———. *Ethics*. In *A Spinoza Reader: The Ethics and Other Works*, translated by Edwin Curley. Princeton: Princeton University Press, 1996, 85–265.

———. "Political Treatise." In *A Theologico-Political Treatise and a Political Treatise*, edited by Francesco Cordasco. New York: Courier Corporation, 2013.

———. *The Principles of Cartesian Philosophy: With, Metaphysical Thoughts*. Edited by Samuel Shirley. New York, Hackett Publishing, 1998.

———. *Theological-Political Treatise*. Cambridge, Cambridge University Press, 2007.

———. "The Treatise on the Emendation of the Intellect." In *Ethics: With The Treatise on the Emendation of the Intellect and Selected Letters*, translated by Samuel Shirley. Indianapolis: Hackett Publishing, 1992.

Westphal, Merold. "Hegel between Spinoza and Derrida." In *Hegel's History of Philosophy: New Interpretations*, edited by David Duquette. Albany, NY: State of New York Press, 2003.

Wolf, Abraham. "Spinoza's Conception of Attributes." In *Studies in Spinoza, Critical and Interpretive Essays*, edited by S. Paul Kashap. California: University of California Press, 1972.

THE MACAT LIBRARY
BY DISCIPLINE

AFRICANA STUDIES

Chinua Achebe's *An Image of Africa: Racism in Conrad's Heart of Darkness*
W. E. B. Du Bois's *The Souls of Black Folk*
Zora Neale Huston's *Characteristics of Negro Expression*
Martin Luther King Jr's *Why We Can't Wait*
Toni Morrison's *Playing in the Dark: Whiteness in the American Literary Imagination*

ANTHROPOLOGY

Arjun Appadurai's *Modernity at Large: Cultural Dimensions of Globalisation*
Philippe Ariès's *Centuries of Childhood*
Franz Boas's *Race, Language and Culture*
Kim Chan & Renée Mauborgne's *Blue Ocean Strategy*
Jared Diamond's *Guns, Germs & Steel: the Fate of Human Societies*
Jared Diamond's *Collapse: How Societies Choose to Fail or Survive*
E. E. Evans-Pritchard's *Witchcraft, Oracles and Magic Among the Azande*
James Ferguson's *The Anti-Politics Machine*
Clifford Geertz's *The Interpretation of Cultures*
David Graeber's *Debt: the First 5000 Years*
Karen Ho's *Liquidated: An Ethnography of Wall Street*
Geert Hofstede's *Culture's Consequences: Comparing Values, Behaviors, Institutes and Organizations across Nations*
Claude Lévi-Strauss's *Structural Anthropology*
Jay Macleod's *Ain't No Makin' It: Aspirations and Attainment in a Low-Income Neighborhood*
Saba Mahmood's *The Politics of Piety: The Islamic Revival and the Feminist Subjec*t
Marcel Mauss's *The Gift*

BUSINESS

Jean Lave & Etienne Wenger's *Situated Learning*
Theodore Levitt's *Marketing Myopia*
Burton G. Malkiel's *A Random Walk Down Wall Street*
Douglas McGregor's *The Human Side of Enterprise*
Michael Porter's *Competitive Strategy: Creating and Sustaining Superior Performance*
John Kotter's *Leading Change*
C. K. Prahalad & Gary Hamel's *The Core Competence of the Corporation*

CRIMINOLOGY

Michelle Alexander's *The New Jim Crow: Mass Incarceration in the Age of Colorblindness*
Michael R. Gottfredson & Travis Hirschi's *A General Theory of Crime*
Richard Herrnstein & Charles A. Murray's *The Bell Curve: Intelligence and Class Structure in American Life*
Elizabeth Loftus's *Eyewitness Testimony*
Jay Macleod's *Ain't No Makin' It: Aspirations and Attainment in a Low-Income Neighborhood*
Philip Zimbardo's *The Lucifer Fffect*

ECONOMICS

Janet Abu-Lughod's *Before European Hegemony*
Ha-Joon Chang's *Kicking Away the Ladder*
David Brion Davis's *The Problem of Slavery in the Age of Revolution*
Milton Friedman's *The Role of Monetary Policy*
Milton Friedman's *Capitalism and Freedom*
David Graeber's *Debt: the First 5000 Years*
Friedrich Hayek's *The Road to Serfdom*
Karen Ho's *Liquidated: An Ethnography of Wall Street*

The Macat Library By Discipline

John Maynard Keynes's *The General Theory of Employment, Interest and Money*
Charles P. Kindleberger's *Manias, Panics and Crashes*
Robert Lucas's *Why Doesn't Capital Flow from Rich to Poor Countries?*
Burton G. Malkiel's *A Random Walk Down Wall Street*
Thomas Robert Malthus's *An Essay on the Principle of Population*
Karl Marx's *Capital*
Thomas Piketty's *Capital in the Twenty-First Century*
Amartya Sen's *Development as Freedom*
Adam Smith's *The Wealth of Nations*
Nassim Nicholas Taleb's *The Black Swan: The Impact of the Highly Improbable*
Amos Tversky's & Daniel Kahneman's *Judgment under Uncertainty: Heuristics and Biases*
Mahbub Ul Haq's *Reflections on Human Development*
Max Weber's *The Protestant Ethic and the Spirit of Capitalism*

FEMINISM AND GENDER STUDIES

Judith Butler's *Gender Trouble*
Simone De Beauvoir's *The Second Sex*
Michel Foucault's *History of Sexuality*
Betty Friedan's *The Feminine Mystique*
Saba Mahmood's *The Politics of Piety: The Islamic Revival and the Feminist Subjec*t
Joan Wallach Scott's *Gender and the Politics of History*
Mary Wollstonecraft's *A Vindication of the Rights of Woman*
Virginia Woolf's *A Room of One's Own*

GEOGRAPHY

The Brundtland Report's *Our Common Future*
Rachel Carson's *Silent Spring*
Charles Darwin's *On the Origin of Species*
James Ferguson's *The Anti-Politics Machine*
Jane Jacobs's *The Death and Life of Great American Cities*
James Lovelock's *Gaia: A New Look on Life on Earth*
Amartya Sen's *Development as Freedom*
Mathis Wackernagel & William Rees's *Our Ecological Footprint*

HISTORY

Janet Abu-Lughod's *Before European Hegemony*
Benedict Anderson's *Imagined Communities*
Bernard Bailyn's *The Ideological Origins of the American Revolution*
Hanna Batatu's *The Old Social Classes And The Revolutionary Movements Of Iraq*
Christopher Browning's *Ordinary Men: Reserve Police Batallion 101 and the Final Solution in Poland*
Edmund Burke's *Reflections on the Revolution in France*
William Cronon's *Nature's Metropolis: Chicago And The Great West*
Alfred W. Crosby's *The Columbian Exchange*
Hamid Dabashi's *Iran: A People Interrupted*
David Brion Davis's *The Problem of Slavery in the Age of Revolution*
Nathalie Zemon Davis's *The Return of Martin Guerre*
Jared Diamond's *Guns, Germs & Steel: the Fate of Human Societies*
Frank Dikotter's *Mao's Great Famine*
John W Dower's *War Without Mercy: Race And Power In The Pacific War*
W. E. B. Du Bois's *The Souls of Black Folk*
Richard J. Evans's *In Defence of History*
Lucien Febvre's *The Problem of Unbelief in the 16th Century*
Sheila Fitzpatrick's *Everyday Stalinism*

Eric Foner's *Reconstruction: America's Unfinished Revolution, 1863-1877*
Michel Foucault's *Discipline and Punish*
Michel Foucault's *History of Sexuality*
Francis Fukuyama's *The End of History and the Last Man*
John Lewis Gaddis's *We Now Know: Rethinking Cold War History*
Ernest Gellner's *Nations and Nationalism*
Eugene Genovese's *Roll, Jordan, Roll: The World the Slaves Made*
Carlo Ginzburg's *The Night Battles*
Daniel Goldhagen's *Hitler's Willing Executioners*
Jack Goldstone's *Revolution and Rebellion in the Early Modern World*
Antonio Gramsci's *The Prison Notebooks*
Alexander Hamilton, John Jay & James Madison's *The Federalist Papers*
Christopher Hill's *The World Turned Upside Down*
Carole Hillenbrand's *The Crusades: Islamic Perspectives*
Thomas Hobbes's *Leviathan*
Eric Hobsbawm's *The Age Of Revolution*
John A. Hobson's *Imperialism: A Study*
Albert Hourani's *History of the Arab Peoples*
Samuel P. Huntington's *The Clash of Civilizations and the Remaking of World Order*
C. L. R. James's *The Black Jacobins*
Tony Judt's *Postwar: A History of Europe Since 1945*
Ernst Kantorowicz's *The King's Two Bodies: A Study in Medieval Political Theology*
Paul Kennedy's *The Rise and Fall of the Great Powers*
Ian Kershaw's *The "Hitler Myth": Image and Reality in the Third Reich*
John Maynard Keynes's *The General Theory of Employment, Interest and Money*
Charles P. Kindleberger's *Manias, Panics and Crashes*
Martin Luther King Jr's *Why We Can't Wait*
Henry Kissinger's *World Order: Reflections on the Character of Nations and the Course of History*
Thomas Kuhn's *The Structure of Scientific Revolutions*
Georges Lefebvre's *The Coming of the French Revolution*
John Locke's *Two Treatises of Government*
Niccolò Machiavelli's *The Prince*
Thomas Robert Malthus's *An Essay on the Principle of Population*
Mahmood Mamdani's *Citizen and Subject: Contemporary Africa And The Legacy Of Late Colonialism*
Karl Marx's *Capital*
Stanley Milgram's *Obedience to Authority*
John Stuart Mill's *On Liberty*
Thomas Paine's *Common Sense*
Thomas Paine's *Rights of Man*
Geoffrey Parker's *Global Crisis: War, Climate Change and Catastrophe in the Seventeenth Century*
Jonathan Riley-Smith's *The First Crusade and the Idea of Crusading*
Jean Jacques Rousseau's *The Social Contract*
Joan Wallach Scott's *Gender and the Politics of History*
Theda Skocpol's *States and Social Revolutions*
Adam Smith's *The Wealth of Nations*
Timothy Snyder's *Bloodlands: Europe Between Hitler and Stalin*
Sun Tzu's *The Art of War*
Keith Thomas's *Religion and the Decline of Magic*
Thucydides's *The History of the Peloponnesian War*
Frederick Jackson Turner's *The Significance of the Frontier in American History*
Odd Arne Westad's *The Global Cold War: Third World Interventions And The Making Of Our Times*

The Macat Library By Discipline

LITERATURE

Chinua Achebe's *An Image of Africa: Racism in Conrad's Heart of Darkness*
Roland Barthes's *Mythologies*
Homi K. Bhabha's *The Location of Culture*
Judith Butler's *Gender Trouble*
Simone De Beauvoir's *The Second Sex*
Ferdinand De Saussure's *Course in General Linguistics*
T. S. Eliot's *The Sacred Wood: Essays on Poetry and Criticism*
Zora Neale Huston's *Characteristics of Negro Expression*
Toni Morrison's *Playing in the Dark: Whiteness in the American Literary Imagination*
Edward Said's *Orientalism*
Gayatri Chakravorty Spivak's *Can the Subaltern Speak?*
Mary Wollstonecraft's *A Vindication of the Rights of Women*
Virginia Woolf's *A Room of One's Own*

PHILOSOPHY

Elizabeth Anscombe's *Modern Moral Philosophy*
Hannah Arendt's *The Human Condition*
Aristotle's *Metaphysics*
Aristotle's *Nicomachean Ethics*
Edmund Gettier's *Is Justified True Belief Knowledge?*
Georg Wilhelm Friedrich Hegel's *Phenomenology of Spirit*
David Hume's *Dialogues Concerning Natural Religion*
David Hume's *The Enquiry for Human Understanding*
Immanuel Kant's *Religion within the Boundaries of Mere Reason*
Immanuel Kant's *Critique of Pure Reason*
Søren Kierkegaard's *The Sickness Unto Death*
Søren Kierkegaard's *Fear and Trembling*
C. S. Lewis's *The Abolition of Man*
Alasdair MacIntyre's *After Virtue*
Marcus Aurelius's *Meditations*
Friedrich Nietzsche's *On the Genealogy of Morality*
Friedrich Nietzsche's *Beyond Good and Evil*
Plato's *Republic*
Plato's *Symposium*
Jean-Jacques Rousseau's *The Social Contract*
Gilbert Ryle's *The Concept of Mind*
Baruch Spinoza's *Ethics*
Sun Tzu's *The Art of War*
Ludwig Wittgenstein's *Philosophical Investigations*

POLITICS

Benedict Anderson's *Imagined Communities*
Aristotle's *Politics*
Bernard Bailyn's *The Ideological Origins of the American Revolution*
Edmund Burke's *Reflections on the Revolution in France*
John C. Calhoun's *A Disquisition on Government*
Ha-Joon Chang's *Kicking Away the Ladder*
Hamid Dabashi's *Iran: A People Interrupted*
Hamid Dabashi's *Theology of Discontent: The Ideological Foundation of the Islamic Revolution in Iran*
Robert Dahl's *Democracy and its Critics*
Robert Dahl's *Who Governs?*
David Brion Davis's *The Problem of Slavery in the Age of Revolution*

Alexis De Tocqueville's *Democracy in America*
James Ferguson's *The Anti-Politics Machine*
Frank Dikotter's *Mao's Great Famine*
Sheila Fitzpatrick's *Everyday Stalinism*
Eric Foner's *Reconstruction: America's Unfinished Revolution, 1863-1877*
Milton Friedman's *Capitalism and Freedom*
Francis Fukuyama's *The End of History and the Last Man*
John Lewis Gaddis's *We Now Know: Rethinking Cold War History*
Ernest Gellner's *Nations and Nationalism*
David Graeber's *Debt: the First 5000 Years*
Antonio Gramsci's *The Prison Notebooks*
Alexander Hamilton, John Jay & James Madison's *The Federalist Papers*
Friedrich Hayek's *The Road to Serfdom*
Christopher Hill's *The World Turned Upside Down*
Thomas Hobbes's *Leviathan*
John A. Hobson's *Imperialism: A Study*
Samuel P. Huntington's *The Clash of Civilizations and the Remaking of World Order*
Tony Judt's *Postwar: A History of Europe Since 1945*
David C. Kang's *China Rising: Peace, Power and Order in East Asia*
Paul Kennedy's *The Rise and Fall of Great Powers*
Robert Keohane's *After Hegemony*
Martin Luther King Jr.'s *Why We Can't Wait*
Henry Kissinger's *World Order: Reflections on the Character of Nations and the Course of History*
John Locke's *Two Treatises of Government*
Niccolò Machiavelli's *The Prince*
Thomas Robert Malthus's *An Essay on the Principle of Population*
Mahmood Mamdani's *Citizen and Subject: Contemporary Africa And The Legacy Of Late Colonialism*
Karl Marx's *Capital*
John Stuart Mill's *On Liberty*
John Stuart Mill's *Utilitarianism*
Hans Morgenthau's *Politics Among Nations*
Thomas Paine's *Common Sense*
Thomas Paine's *Rights of Man*
Thomas Piketty's *Capital in the Twenty-First Century*
Robert D. Putman's *Bowling Alone*
John Rawls's *Theory of Justice*
Jean-Jacques Rousseau's *The Social Contract*
Theda Skocpol's *States and Social Revolutions*
Adam Smith's *The Wealth of Nations*
Sun Tzu's *The Art of War*
Henry David Thoreau's *Civil Disobedience*
Thucydides's *The History of the Peloponnesian War*
Kenneth Waltz's *Theory of International Politics*
Max Weber's *Politics as a Vocation*
Odd Arne Westad's *The Global Cold War: Third World Interventions And The Making Of Our Times*

POSTCOLONIAL STUDIES

Roland Barthes's *Mythologies*
Frantz Fanon's *Black Skin, White Masks*
Homi K. Bhabha's *The Location of Culture*
Gustavo Gutiérrez's *A Theology of Liberation*
Edward Said's *Orientalism*
Gayatri Chakravorty Spivak's *Can the Subaltern Speak?*

The Macat Library By Discipline

PSYCHOLOGY

Gordon Allport's *The Nature of Prejudice*
Alan Baddeley & Graham Hitch's *Aggression: A Social Learning Analysis*
Albert Bandura's *Aggression: A Social Learning Analysis*
Leon Festinger's *A Theory of Cognitive Dissonance*
Sigmund Freud's *The Interpretation of Dreams*
Betty Friedan's *The Feminine Mystique*
Michael R. Gottfredson & Travis Hirschi's *A General Theory of Crime*
Eric Hoffer's *The True Believer: Thoughts on the Nature of Mass Movements*
William James's *Principles of Psychology*
Elizabeth Loftus's *Eyewitness Testimony*
A. H. Maslow's *A Theory of Human Motivation*
Stanley Milgram's *Obedience to Authority*
Steven Pinker's *The Better Angels of Our Nature*
Oliver Sacks's *The Man Who Mistook His Wife For a Hat*
Richard Thaler & Cass Sunstein's *Nudge: Improving Decisions About Health, Wealth and Happiness*
Amos Tversky's *Judgment under Uncertainty: Heuristics and Biases*
Philip Zimbardo's *The Lucifer Effect*

SCIENCE

Rachel Carson's *Silent Spring*
William Cronon's *Nature's Metropolis: Chicago And The Great West*
Alfred W. Crosby's *The Columbian Exchange*
Charles Darwin's *On the Origin of Species*
Richard Dawkin's *The Selfish Gene*
Thomas Kuhn's *The Structure of Scientific Revolutions*
Geoffrey Parker's *Global Crisis: War, Climate Change and Catastrophe in the Seventeenth Century*
Mathis Wackernagel & William Rees's *Our Ecological Footprint*

SOCIOLOGY

Michelle Alexander's *The New Jim Crow: Mass Incarceration in the Age of Colorblindness*
Gordon Allport's *The Nature of Prejudice*
Albert Bandura's *Aggression: A Social Learning Analysis*
Hanna Batatu's *The Old Social Classes And The Revolutionary Movements Of Iraq*
Ha-Joon Chang's *Kicking Away the Ladder*
W. E. B. Du Bois's *The Souls of Black Folk*
Émile Durkheim's *On Suicide*
Frantz Fanon's *Black Skin, White Masks*
Frantz Fanon's *The Wretched of the Earth*
Eric Foner's *Reconstruction: America's Unfinished Revolution, 1863-1877*
Eugene Genovese's *Roll, Jordan, Roll: The World the Slaves Made*
Jack Goldstone's *Revolution and Rebellion in the Early Modern World*
Antonio Gramsci's *The Prison Notebooks*
Richard Herrnstein & Charles A Murray's *The Bell Curve: Intelligence and Class Structure in American Life*
Eric Hoffer's *The True Believer: Thoughts on the Nature of Mass Movements*
Jane Jacobs's *The Death and Life of Great American Cities*
Robert Lucas's *Why Doesn't Capital Flow from Rich to Poor Countries?*
Jay Macleod's *Ain't No Makin' It: Aspirations and Attainment in a Low Income Neighborhood*
Elaine May's *Homeward Bound: American Families in the Cold War Era*
Douglas McGregor's *The Human Side of Enterprise*
C. Wright Mills's *The Sociological Imagination*

Thomas Piketty's *Capital in the Twenty-First Century*
Robert D. Putman's *Bowling Alone*
David Riesman's *The Lonely Crowd: A Study of the Changing American Character*
Edward Said's *Orientalism*
Joan Wallach Scott's *Gender and the Politics of History*
Theda Skocpol's *States and Social Revolutions*
Max Weber's *The Protestant Ethic and the Spirit of Capitalism*

THEOLOGY

Augustine's *Confessions*
Benedict's *Rule of St Benedict*
Gustavo Gutiérrez's *A Theology of Liberation*
Carole Hillenbrand's *The Crusades: Islamic Perspectives*
David Hume's *Dialogues Concerning Natural Religion*
Immanuel Kant's *Religion within the Boundaries of Mere Reason*
Ernst Kantorowicz's *The King's Two Bodies: A Study in Medieval Political Theology*
Søren Kierkegaard's *The Sickness Unto Death*
C. S. Lewis's *The Abolition of Man*
Saba Mahmood's *The Politics of Piety: The Islamic Revival and the Feminist Subjec*t
Baruch Spinoza's *Ethics*
Keith Thomas's *Religion and the Decline of Magic*

COMING SOON

Chris Argyris's *The Individual and the Organisation*
Seyla Benhabib's *The Rights of Others*
Walter Benjamin's *The Work Of Art in the Age of Mechanical Reproduction*
John Berger's *Ways of Seeing*
Pierre Bourdieu's *Outline of a Theory of Practice*
Mary Douglas's *Purity and Danger*
Roland Dworkin's *Taking Rights Seriously*
James G. March's *Exploration and Exploitation in Organisational Learning*
Ikujiro Nonaka's *A Dynamic Theory of Organizational Knowledge Creation*
Griselda Pollock's *Vision and Difference*
Amartya Sen's *Inequality Re-Examined*
Susan Sontag's *On Photography*
Yasser Tabbaa's *The Transformation of Islamic Art*
Ludwig von Mises's *Theory of Money and Credit*

Printed in the United States
by Baker & Taylor Publisher Services